He grasped her hand and, pressing it against his cheek, gently kissed each finger. "I am and always will be yours. Do you know I would have searched for you for the rest of my life? I was frantic with worry."

"I'm sorry," she began.

He silenced her by closing his eyes and giving a slight shake of his head. "All is forgiven. I understand."

Lauren felt a huge weight lifting from her. It dawned on her that they were finally together. How many times had she dreamed of meeting KC face to face? Of looking into his eyes and feeling his arms around her? It had never been like this in her vivid imaginings that obviously were not as creative as God's. *This,* she decided, *is what falling in love is supposed to feel like.*

Palisades.
Pure Romance.

Fiction that features credible characters and
entertaining plot lines, while continuing to uphold
strong Christian values. From high adventure
to tender stories of the heart, each Palisades
Romance is an undiluted story of love,
from beginning to end!

ECHOES

ROBIN JONES GUNN

ECHOES
published by Palisades
a part of the Questar publishing family
© 1996 by Robin Jones Gunn
International Standard Book Number: 0-88070-773-9

Cover illustration by George Angelini
Cover designed by David Carlson and
Mona Weir-Daly
Edited by Janet Kobobel Grant

Most Scripture quotations are from: *The New King James Version*
©1984 by Thomas Nelson, Inc.

Also quoted:

The Living Bible (TLB) ©1971 by Tyndale House Publishers

Printed in the United States of America

Library of Congress Cataloging-in-Publication Data
Gunn, Robin Jones, 1955-
    Echoes / Robin Jones Gunn.   p.   cm.
    "A Palisades contemporary romance."
    ISBN: 0-88070-773-9 (alk. paper)
    I. Title.   PS3557.U4866E26   1996
    813'.54--dc20   96-19005   CIP

98 99 00 01 02 03 — 10 9 8 7 6 5 4 3

For Ross,
the other half of my heart,
who said all the right things
when I came home after a perm disaster.

The voice of the LORD echoes from the clouds.
The God of glory thunders through the skies.

PSALMS 29:3

One

❧

Lauren Phillips flipped the magazine page and stopped. There it was: The garden gazebo she had been trying to describe to Jeff.

"Would it be okay if I tore this page out?" she asked the hairdresser who stood over her, busily unrolling the perm rods from Lauren's long hair.

"Sure. That's an old copy. Did you find a good recipe?"

"No, I found a gazebo." She held up the picture. "This is where I want to get married."

"Romantic," the stylist commented, tugging out another rod. "Looks like the one at Belmont."

Lauren had heard about Belmont University and the 150-year-old mansion on the campus that was available for wedding rentals. She would have to look into that.

The stylist continued working on Lauren's blond hair. "Gazebos aren't especially practical for weddings, you know. Where do all the guests sit?"

Jeff asked the same question last week when she tried to describe the gazebo setting to him. "I haven't figured that out yet," she glanced at her watch. "Do you think this will take much longer?" For nearly four hours she had endured the torture of getting a perm. Her tender head was protesting the treatment, and Jeff would be waiting at the restaurant. He didn't like to be kept waiting.

"Almost done."

Lauren nervously twisted the large diamond ring on her finger and wondered why she ever thought getting a spiral perm was a good idea. It was her first perm since she was fourteen. Since that experience ten years ago, she had worn her silky blond hair the same way — straight down her back, hanging almost to her waist. Then, a few weeks ago, Lauren's supervisor at the bank had come to this salon during her lunch hour. She was transformed from drab to dynamite and that had convinced Lauren to live a little and surprise Jeff with a new look.

With a yank, the stylist pulled out the final rod and maneuvered a wide pick through Lauren's long locks. Suddenly the comb-out stopped, and in a thin voice the stylist called for her supervisor. He joined her, and the two seemed to talk in code, both touching the ends of Lauren's hair and pulling their fingers through the underside. She wished they would spin her chair around so she could have a look in the mirror.

"Have you been in the pool a lot this summer?" the supervisor asked.

"No." *It was only the end of June. Why would he ask such a question?*

"We'll include a bottle of our 911 conditioner for you to use at home," he said. "Wait two days before you wash your hair."

Lauren noticed as he walked away that strands of her blond hair were between his fingers.

"What's wrong with my hair?" Lauren turned herself around to face the mirror before the stylist could stop her. The sight of her reflection was shocking. Instead of soft waves of caramel cascading down, as shown on the model in the *Hairstyles for Today* book, Lauren's hair had turned into wild, crumpled straw, zigzagging from the crown of her head.

"What happened?" she cried.

"Sometimes it takes a day or two for the perm to calm down," the woman said brightly. "You need to give it a little time to relax. Be sure to use the conditioner."

"This is not what I wanted," Lauren said. She fingered the dry ends of her hair and ran her hand over the back. "It's... it's not what I wanted. I want my old hair back."

The stylist unclasped the drape from around Lauren's neck and said, "It should relax in a few days."

Lauren reached for her backpack and walked the ten feet to the register, certain the customers waiting in the front of the shop would all look up at her and burst into laughter.

"Here you go," the manager said, handing her the conditioner. "And I gave you a 20 percent discount."

"A 20 percent discount? Why?"

"As a courtesy, that's all."

Lauren was too numb to ask any more questions. She signed the Visa voucher and filled in the tip portion of the form with a hastily figured 15 percent. "Thank you," she mumbled, bolting for the parking lot.

Why did I leave her a tip? She probably ruined my hair! That's why they gave me the discount. I can't believe this happened!

Lauren quickly unlocked her door, slid into the driver's

seat, and jerked the rearview mirror in her direction.

"Oh, no. No, no, no!" she moaned. "My poor hair! What am I going to do?" She ran her fingers through the clump of hair hanging over her shoulder, and a dozen strands came out. A repeat finger-combing brought out more hair.

Fighting back the tears, Lauren jammed the keys into the ignition and popped her Taurus into reverse. She backed out of the tight parking space. The sound of tires screeching caused her to automatically slam on her brakes. With the rearview mirror still askew, Lauren turned to look over her shoulder and discovered she had missed hitting another car by mere inches.

"Sorry!" Lauren called, rolling down her window and signaling her apology to the woman in the other car. The motorist shook her head at Lauren and sped off. "I said I was sorry," Lauren muttered, pausing to adjust her rearview mirror. Then, with extra caution, she exited the Hickory Hollow Mall parking lot.

Nearly fifteen minutes later she arrived across town at Giovanni's Italian Restaurant. She had to circle the block twice to find a parking place. Before jumping out of the car, Lauren scrounged around in her backpack for a barrette, a scrunchie, a rubber band, anything to pull back her hair. She found a long wooden clip and tried to clasp her hair into a ponytail. It was too thick now for the clip. Quickly dividing her hair into three sections, she loosely twisted it into a braid down her back, securing the clip on the end. Another wad of hair came out in her hand.

My hair is ruined! This was supposed to be my big surprise for Jeff, and here I am, almost an hour late, and with my hair falling out!

Lauren entered the Italian restaurant and inhaled the familiar garlic fragrance. She and Jeff met here often. There was something slightly soothing about the surroundings. Lauren spotted Jeff in "their" corner booth and wove her way through the maze of tables.

"Jeff, I am so sorry," she began.

He looked up and said nothing. His deep brown eyes greeted her flatly, and his straight lips gave no hint of what he was thinking. She hated it when Jeff was like this. As long as she had known him he had only turned stoic a couple of times, but when he did, trying to get him to open up was like digging a ditch with a teaspoon.

Lauren slipped into the seat across from Jeff and cautiously asked, "Have you ordered already?"

"No. I was waiting."

"I'm sorry I'm so late. You won't believe what happened."

The waiter stepped up to the table with his pencil poised on his order pad. "Have you had time to decide?"

"I'll have the special, whatever it is tonight," Lauren said.

"Lasagna," Jeff ordered without taking his eyes off of Lauren. He always ordered lasagna at Giovanni's. That was one of the things Lauren loved about him. Jeff was steady. Predictable. Dependable. Qualities she wanted and needed in a man.

Lauren used to order the same thing every time, too. Then about two weeks ago, she suddenly grew sick of lasagna. She decided to order things on the menu that she couldn't even pronounce. It was that "live dangerously" attitude that had prompted her to make the appointment at the hair salon.

"Jeff," she tried again, "you won't believe what happened."

Lauren flipped her braid over her shoulder and tried to appear lighthearted about the perm disaster. Several stray hairs floated onto her arm. "I wanted to surprise you. Marie at work — did you ever meet her? She's my supervisor. Well, anyway, she went to this salon a few weeks ago, and her hair turned out gorgeous. So I decided to do something different with my hair. I went in at two-thirty today. Can you believe it? It took more than four hours for them to give me this perm. You should've seen me with all those rods in my hair. It stuck out to here." She used her hands to demonstrate. Jeff gave her a polite smile.

"And now I have to wait before I can wash it. I have some good conditioner to use that should help the dryness. It got pretty dried out." She smiled, trying to convince herself and Jeff that everything would turn out okay once she got home and washed her hair.

"Things always seem to happen to you, Lauren," Jeff said.

She ignored his comment. Other people had said the same thing to her over the years. It was true. But she didn't like the image it gave of her being a disaster magnet. "I was tired of having long, straight, boring hair. It was time for a change. You'll like it. Just wait. You'll see."

"I liked it the way it was," Jeff said.

Lauren took a sip from her water glass. "So," she said, still forcing the cheery tone into her words, "what's been happening with you? You didn't call me last night. Did you have to work late? Did you guys land that account with Harrison Furniture?"

Jeff worked as a marketing specialist for Anchor Advertising in Nashville, and for the last three weeks he had talked about the Harrison Furniture account as being the one that would open doors for him to move up in the company. Jeff was a hard worker, and it was important to him to move up. Earlier that week Jeff had said the Harrison account was a sure thing. This evening he wasn't responding to Lauren's questions. He drank the last of his Diet Coke, and with three fingers motioned for the waiter to bring him another. Lauren reached across the table and took Jeff's cool hand in hers.

"Are you all right?"

"Another Diet Coke, sir?" the waiter inquired. Jeff nodded.

"I'll be right back with that. And your dinners should be about ready."

Lauren held Jeff's hand tighter as he seemed to be slipping away from her. "I found a picture of the gazebo I was trying to explain to you. And the hairdresser said there was a really nice gazebo at Belmont. Have you ever seen it? Maybe we should go over there sometime and have a look."

"One lasagna," the waiter said, placing the steaming boat-shaped plate in front of Jeff. "And one special."

Lauren let go of Jeff's hand and smiled at the waiter. Her gaze followed the white plate as he set it before her. Her smile vanished. "Excuse me," she said as he was turning to go. "What is this?"

"Eggplant parmigiana with scallops in garlic sauce."

"Oh, no," Lauren muttered.

"You ordered the special, right?"

"Yes, but I didn't know what it was. I should have asked. You see, I'm allergic to scallops. I ate some once when I was a child, and I ended up in the hospital. They make my throat constrict." Lauren pinched at her throat for emphasis and let out a nervous laugh. "I know it's strange, but that's what happens. Would it be possible to change my order?"

"What would you like?" the waiter asked.

"I guess lasagna would be fine."

He reached for the plate and repeated, "One lasagna. I'll bring you a basket of bread as well."

"Thank you." Lauren kept her gaze on the waiter a little longer than necessary. She was hesitant to look back at Jeff. Jeff didn't like "scenes" in public places. Or in private places, for that matter. He was very good about making sure everything appeared calm and unruffled on the outside. She liked that about him. It was one of the strengths that drew her to him when they met. Lauren had grown up with a rather opinionated step-father who embarrassed her more than once in public. She vowed she would never marry a man who couldn't be polite in public. Jeff was always polite.

"Sorry," she offered meekly when her gaze returned to the table.

She caught Jeff's eye only briefly, hating this feeling of needing to defend herself to him. How could she explain why she thought it was a good idea to order the special? Or why it seemed logical to get her hair permed? Or why she was trying new things all of a sudden? She didn't have a reason. At least not one that she understood. Something inside of her was not happy with the way her life was going, and she was eager to talk it through with Jeff. Being a good listener was another one of Jeff's terrific qualities. Lauren knew, though, that for a topic this complex and deep, she had to wait until they were alone. Jeff didn't discuss such things in public.

He reached for her hand and, squeezing it, said, "Don't worry about it."

She gave him a wobbly smile and said, "Thanks for understanding."

"That's what I do best."

The lasagna arrived, and their meal continued quietly, each of them lost in thought. Jeff talked about a new place he had found that had tuned up his car that morning. He mentioned that he was thinking of having the seats of his sedan reupholstered in leather. Lauren listened, smiled, nodded appropriately, and ate her lasagna without any comments. She was eager to get to her apartment where they could really talk.

Lauren arrived at her apartment before Jeff. She started the coffee and turned on the stereo, choosing one of Jeff's favorite CDs. Kicking off her tennis shoes, Lauren stretched out on her sofa and waited for Jeff's familiar footsteps up the stairs to her apartment. A week ago she had revamped her beat-up garage-sale couch with a rose and hunter green floral cover she had ordered from a catalog. It came with three matching pillows and a rose colored cover which perfectly fit her overstuffed chair.

The new look had transformed her small apartment and made her eager to do some more decorating, letting her artistic side have some fun. She had one end table at the foot of the sofa. It was a rich cherry-wood piece with thin, spindled legs and one drawer with a brass latch. She had snagged it for fifteen bucks at a sidewalk sale because one of the back legs was broken. Jeff had told her to save up for a quality piece of furniture, but she had taken pity on the three-legged table, repaired it with a hot glue gun, and as far as she was concerned, the table was as good as new.

The front door knocker clapped twice. Jeff's knock.

"Come on in," she called and rose to meet him. It was evenings like this when Lauren felt as if she and Jeff were already married. They would drink their french roast together from oversized mugs, sharing their favorite hazelnut coffee creamer and talking until the early hours, planning their future together. It was all calm, steady, and predictable.

Jeff entered with a bouquet of daisies. He had probably purchased them from the young boy who stood on the corner three blocks away, peddling his wares each summer evening.

"How pretty!" Lauren gave him a kiss on the cheek and took the flowers from him. "You're so sweet."

Jeff reached out and drew her to him. He wrapped his arms around her slim frame and buried his face against the side of her hair. His tender embrace lasted only a moment. "What's that smell?"

"The coffee?"

"No, your hair."

"Oh. It's the perm solution. It'll wash out."

"Didn't you say you have to wait before you wash your hair?"

"Two days. But maybe I can wash it tomorrow. It might help it," Lauren said, turning to get a vase from the kitchen counter. She clipped the daisies' ends and dropped them into her favorite royal blue glass vase. They brightened up the whole kitchen.

"How do you like the furniture covers?" she asked as Jeff poured the coffee.

He looked over at the new ensemble and said one word. "Pink?"

"It's not pink. It's rose. Mauve, actually. It's the Victorian look."

"I think it looks pink."

"Don't you like it?"

"Do you?" Jeff countered.

"Of course I do."

"It's just that sometimes you order things you don't really like but you keep them anyway."

"When did that ever happen? Name one time," Lauren challenged, her hand on her hip.

"You know what?" Jeff said, adding cream to the two mugs of coffee. "It doesn't matter. As long as you're happy with it, that's all that counts." He walked away from her with his mug in his hand, leaving hers on the counter. Then, as if he were being defiant about having anything to do with her choice of a "pink" furniture cover, he went over and sat on the floor, leaning his back against the easy chair.

"You can sit on it," Lauren said, grabbing her mug and joining him.

"I'm fine right here," he said.

Lauren settled herself comfortably on her Victorian sofa, propped a pillow under her arm and said, "So tell me what's going on with the Harrison Furniture account."

Jeff sipped his coffee and took his time before saying, "I'm unemployed."

Lauren thought he was joking. "What are you saying? Did Granddaddy Harrison reject the jingle again?"

"Lauren, I was let go yesterday."

She slowly lowered her mug and met his eyes. "Jeff, I'm so sorry. I didn't know. Why didn't you tell me? What happened?"

"Anchor was bought out. Nobody in my division knew about it. They're consolidating with a firm from South

Carolina, and both companies will be part of Burrows, James, and Tompkins in New York. Everyone from my department was let go except Garry."

"Garry? Why Garry? He's only been working there a few months."

Jeff ran his finger along his mug's rim. "Seems Garry was more or less a corporate spy from the New York agency. He used his three months with us to decide who should stay and who should go. He apparently has a whole new team handpicked for Nashville. I'm not one of them."

"But it sounds as if nobody from your department was one of his choices," Lauren said, not sure if the logic would cheer him up any.

"No," Jeff answered slowly.

"You can find another job in Nashville. The wedding isn't until February. That gives us, what? Eight months? That's plenty of time for you to find a new job."

"It looks as if I already have a new job," Jeff said slowly.

"What?"

"Garry recommended me for a position in New York. I'd be a fool not to take it."

"New York?" Lauren said, sinking deep into her bed of roses. "New York?"

"It's a huge career opportunity for me, Lauren." He leaned forward, looking alive for the first time all night. "You could learn to like New York."

"Jeff, I've been to New York. I don't like it. What about all our plans to move to the country? All along we've been talking about moving out of Nashville after we're married. Remember? Some land with a garden and maybe a guest house out back. We could never live like that in New York."

"Sure we could. They have 'country' homes with vegetable gardens in New York, too."

"No, they don't Jeff. Not for miles and miles. You would have to commute hours every day. And we could never afford to buy a house there. This is…," Lauren put her mug on the floor and dropped her head in her hands. "This is not what we planned."

"You mean not what you planned."

"What do you mean by that?"

Dead air enveloped the gulf between them as Jeff paused, and the CD player mysteriously stopped for thirty seconds before starting the next song. It was one of Jeff's favorites. The song began:

I'm not the kind who takes chances,
But baby, I took a chance on you.
And I'm not saying
You're not worth romancin'
But have we got what it takes
To see us through?

Call me when you wake up
When you smell the coffee
When the scent of roses
Is enough to clear your head
You call me…

"What are you saying, Jeff?" Lauren asked. Inside her a huge wave of emotion was about to crash over her.

"I don't know, Lauren. You tell me. Can you live in New York?"

Two

Monday at lunch Lauren poured out her heart to her friend, Mindy, as they sat in the basement lunch room.

"And that was it?" Mindy asked. "Love me, love New York? End of discussion?"

Swirling her spoon around in her yogurt carton, Lauren lowered her eyes. She and Mindy ate lunch together nearly every day, and on this gloomy Monday Lauren was glad she had someone to talk to. Mindy was a good listener but not always a good empathizer. Probably because her life was normal. Calm. Not bizarre. Crazy things like a perm disaster never seemed to happen to Mindy.

"There was a lot more to the discussion than that," Lauren said. "We talked until almost two in the morning. The thing is, this is Jeff's dream, to work at a New York advertising agency. He thought it would take ten or twelve years before he would be groomed for such a position. I guess he thought by that time we would be married, have a kid or two, and wherever Daddy would go, the family would follow. He said, 'I thought you would have your fling with country living for the first few years of our marriage, and then we could move on.'"

"Oh, the man does not get it, does he? He's thinking you're going to raise your babies in the city? And what? They'll learn what a tree is when the nanny takes them to Central Park once a week? Where is his mind?" Mindy asked, ripping open the wrapper on a package of honey roasted peanuts. "The man is only thinking of himself, which is, of course, a prerequisite for being a man."

Mindy had been married to Leon for almost a year now. He was a gentle giant who taught science at Nelson High and catered to Mindy's every whim. She adored him, and they made a darling couple. Leon was a foot or more taller than Mindy and appeared most content when he stood beside her, his arm resting on her shoulder, showing off his cute little wife to the world. He had reason to feel proud. Mindy was a beautiful woman with glittering dark eyes full of spunk.

"I hope you told Jeffrey to go lay an egg!" Mindy spouted.

"I didn't tell him anything. We're still talking things through. It's very complicated."

"Why should it be complicated? You meet someone, you get to know him, you fall in love, and you get married. What's to work out?"

"Plenty."

"You have my prayers, girlfriend," Mindy said, rising to clear her spot at the employee lunch table and return to work. "You may not have my excellent taste in men, but you have my prayers."

"Thanks. I have a feeling I'll need every bit of them."

Lauren took the elevator up to the first floor with Mindy.

The two of them returned to their teller windows and opened up for their afternoon of nonstop business. The last few days of the month were always the busiest, and this week promised to be a hummer.

Jeff called Lauren on Monday afternoon and asked if she wanted to get together to talk that evening. She told him she needed some more time to think. He said that Garry had asked him to give a final decision by the end of the week. Jeff's final words were, "So if you could try to hurry your part of this decision along, I'd appreciate it."

His words stung. Lauren was not one to decide anything in a snap. She needed time to weigh out all the options, to think through every possible scenario, to make sure the conclusion she ended up with was one she could live with. That's why her hair was such a complex problem for her. She had thought through the idea of a perm for several days before she made the appointment. Then she had postponed the appointment for a week to allow herself time to change her mind. Everything inside her had said to go for it. She had, and the result was a disaster.

If she couldn't trust her judgment on her hair and salon choice, how could she trust her choice of a husband? Or where she would live for the rest of her life? Hadn't her order at Giovanni's taught her the folly of choosing "the special" without considering all the other options? She needed to ask questions. To collect all the facts.

Lauren changed into her most comfortable cotton pajamas and curled up on her flowery sofa. With a pad of paper and pen in hand, she began to list all her options. One of the columns bore the title, "New York." She had been there three times: Once during her childhood to visit her great-aunt

Clarita, who lived in a ritzy apartment; and twice during her teen years — one trip to visit her ailing great-aunt and another trip three months later for Aunt Clarita's funeral. None of her New York excursions had been enjoyable.

Except maybe the second trip, when she and her only sibling, her younger brother Bradley, had been taken to the theater to see *The Phantom of the Opera*. That was a wonderful, memorable night. She was sixteen, almost seventeen, and as innocent as the musical's character Christine. Brad bought the cassette tape, and together they listened to it over and over during the following year.

Then Lauren had gone off to college in California. It was a small, private Christian college, and not a single person she met there had seen *The Phantom*. She enjoyed her pinch of sophistication, as if she and Brad (or as she had nicknamed him, "Rad") shared something the rest of her world was not privy to.

In the "New York" column on her pad of paper, Lauren wrote, "Culture — theater, museums.".

For two hours she worked on her list, skipping dinner and letting her answering machine pick up the two calls that came in. Finally, when she couldn't think of anything else to add in the "pro" or "con" columns, she sat back and took a look. The "cons" outnumbered the "pros" about four to one.

"The fact of the matter is," she said aloud, practicing how she would present her conclusions to Jeff tomorrow night, "I don't think I'm a New York type of person. Not just in regard to living in the city but even life as a commuting family. That's not what I want. I don't like New York or the idea of New York and I..." Her steam sputtered out.

Lauren padded in her slippers to the kitchen and searched

for something to eat in the fridge. She was hungry for Chinese food but settled for a half-full carton of non-fat cottage cheese. "That's another thing, Jeff," she continued her imaginary conversation. "Why do we always have to go to Giovanni's? I like Chinese food, and you don't; so we never get Chinese. We always end up where you want to go. What if I don't like Italian anymore? Would we still eat there because you like it?

"What do I like?" Lauren asked herself, finishing off the cottage cheese and tossing the container in the trash. "I don't know what I like anymore." She thought for a long, silent minute and said aloud, "I think I need a cat."

She had never owned a cat while she was growing up because her step-father said he was allergic to them. The real reason, she was sure, was that he hated cats. The allergy excuse served as a cover-up. Having been deprived of a kitten in childhood, this seemed a good time to obtain one. Lauren didn't know if Jeff liked cats. She would ask him tomorrow night. Maybe if they had to live in an apartment in New York, it would be okay if she had a kitten. One of those fluffy ones.

What am I saying? "If" I lived in New York? Two minutes ago it wasn't even an option!

All the mental debating exhausted Lauren. She headed for bed and in the dark silence of her room whispered her evening prayers. A cheerful chorus of crickets serenaded outside her open window, and a summer breeze, fragrant from the blooming honeysuckle along the back fence of the apartment complex, soothed her to sleep.

In the morning she still didn't have an answer for Jeff. She had prayed her heart out while she dressed, and on the way to work. All her words bounced off the heavens. What Lauren longed for was an echo of reassurance from God that everything was going to turn out okay, that Jeff was really, truly the right man for her, and that all she had to do was move forward in faith. But by Tuesday evening, she still had no confirmation.

Lauren left work flustered. Instead of driving straight home, she took Mindy's advice about her hair problem and stopped at the mall. She marched back to the salon and found the supervisor at the cash register. He seemed to recognize Lauren the minute she walked in because he said, "Did you want to pick up some more conditioner? I have a bottle of 911 right here. No charge."

"No, I don't want a bottle of your conditioner. I'd like my money back. No, actually, I'd like my hair back. Look at this." She pulled her fingers through her hair and showed him the handful of dry strands that resulted.

"Is there a problem here?" An elegant looking woman stepped to the register, taking instant command of the situation.

"I'd like to speak to the manager."

"I'm the manager," the striking woman said. Her soft brown hair was twisted up in a French roll. Her skin and makeup were flawless. "May I help you?"

Lauren had enough frustration stored up to let her feelings rush out. When she finished her discourse, the manager snapped open the drawer of the register, refunded Lauren's money, and said, "If you have time, I'd personally like to give you a deep conditioning treatment. No charge, of course."

Lauren felt relieved that her complaint was being taken seriously. For the next hour, the manager doted on Lauren.

When it came time for the comb-out, the moment of truth, Lauren's hair came out by the handsful.

"Well," the manager said, looking at Lauren's reflection in the mirror, "I didn't want to see that. I'm afraid your hair has been so badly damaged the best thing would be to cut it."

"I don't want my hair cut."

"I understand."

"Can't you fix it?"

"I've tried. The conditioner I used is the best on the market. Your hair is damaged beyond repair. If it's any consolation, the stylist who did your hair no longer works here."

Lauren sat still, gazing at her reflection. Her hair was like a fuzzy halo with thousands of broken strands sticking out all around her head. She felt like saying, "No, that's no consolation at all."

"How much do you have to cut?" Lauren asked.

"Well...," the manager reached for a book and said, "would you like me to make a few suggestions?"

Lauren felt like giving a snappy answer, but the woman was trying to be nice. Letting her eyes fall to the open page where the woman pointed, Lauren didn't reply.

"This cut would look absolutely fantastic on you." She ducked her head, trying to make eye contact with Lauren. "What do you think?"

The picture showed a model with long bangs and hair just below her earlobes. Lauren had never worn bangs. She had always worn her hair long. In every school picture since first grade she had posed with her hair hanging over her shoulders, marking how far her silky blond hair had grown since the previous year. Long hair was her trademark, her identity. It was the thing people always commented on when they first met her. Jeff had said it was what made him want to ask her out. He had admitted one evening, about three months into their relationship, that the first day he saw her he had dreamed about touching her hair. Getting a perm was a major decision. But whacking it all off? How could she ever do that? Who would she be without her golden mane? What would Jeff think? What would he say?

"Hack it," Lauren said in a low rumble.

"You would like me to style your hair like this?" the woman asked.

Lauren nodded, gazing at her reflection. "Quick. Before I change my mind."

Three

Lauren stood before her bedroom mirror, looking at herself this way and that. Her hair was short, all right. Long, thin bangs softly shadowed her forehead. The sides were slicked back with a natural wave exposing her ears while the ends of her hair just touched the top of her collar. The style was flattering to her face. As sullen as she had been at the salon, she now had to admit she liked the haircut.

It was the sight of all her long hair on the floor that had prompted the knot in her stomach. She had found it impossible to thank the manager for the free haircut and style. But at this moment, the change seemed okay. She felt prettier than she had ever felt in her life. Jeff was sure to like it.

The phone rang. Lauren glanced at the clock as she grabbed the phone from its cradle on the kitchen counter. Eight o'clock. It would be Jeff, calling after his racquetball game.

"Are you planning to stop by?" Lauren asked.

"Actually, Garry is with me. We're going to go grab something to eat," Jeff said. "Why don't we get together for dinner tomorrow right after work. Say, six at Giovanni's?"

"Okay, but Jeff?"

"Yes?"

"Would it be all right with you if we went someplace other than Giovanni's for a change?"

"Where do you want to go?" He didn't sound irritated, just surprised.

"I don't know. Maybe for Chinese or Mexican or even to a steak house."

"I'll make reservations at The Ambassador," Jeff said. "Is six still okay?"

"Sure. That's fine." Lauren cringed. The Ambassador was one of the nicest restaurants in town. She didn't mean they had to eat at some place fancy, just some place other than Giovanni's. Also, The Ambassador was only a few blocks from Jeff's office, but it was a twenty-five-minute drive from the bank where Lauren worked. Now she would have to wear something especially nice to work.

"So I'll see you then," Jeff said.

"Oh, Jeff?"

"Yes?"

She didn't know how to tell him about her hair. "Nothing. I'll see you tomorrow at six."

"Okay. Love you. *Ciao.*"

"Love you, too," Lauren said into the receiver as the dial tone began to buzz in her ear. *Ciao?* Since when did Jeff say *ciao?*

Lauren dialed Mindy's number, but the answering machine responded. Lauren left a quick message. "Hi, it's me. I need to talk to you, Min. Call me tonight. It doesn't matter how late. Bye."

Mindy didn't call back. Lauren was ready to chew her out the next morning at work, but when Lauren arrived, Mindy was already in the vault along with the supervisor and two other tellers, checking out cash drawers. When Lauren walked in, they all stopped talking to stare at her.

"What?"

"Lauren?" Mindy was the first to speak. "Look at you, girl!" She balanced her cash drawer on her hip and stepped up for a closer look. "Turn around."

Lauren did. All the other women were silent.

"I love it!" Mindy finally exploded. "You look absolutely fantastic. I can't believe how different you look! And that blue suit...When did you buy that? It makes your eyes look huge and blue as the sea."

The other women joined in with enthusiastic comments: "What a darling style!" "Did you go to the same salon that Marie went to?" "You look so much older. Not older, bad. But older more sophisticated. Your long hair always made you look like a teenager. Now you look..."

Mindy filled in with a movie-star imitation. "Ma'velous, dahling. Simply ma'velous!"

The affirmation did Lauren's heart good. She had set her alarm an hour earlier than usual to allow extra time to shower, work with her hair, and decide on something simple enough for work and yet nice enough for The Ambassador. To her surprise, it took no time to wash and condition her hair. With a blow dryer in one hand and brush in the other, she was able to coax her hair into place immediately. The only tricky part was when she had taken one last brush down the back and instinctively kept brushing even though the hair stopped. A surge of sorrow had welled up. Phantom pains over the missing locks. The rave reviews from her coworkers were exactly what she needed.

"What did Jeff say?" Mindy asked, as they moved to their work stations and began to count out their cash drawers.

"He hasn't seen it yet."

"But you told him, didn't you?"

"I was going to…"

"The man is going to flip! He's going to be afraid to take you to New York now. No doubt a modeling agency will discover you the first day and whisk you away from him. You look great, Lauren. Especially in that color blue. I never noticed how blue your eyes were. They match that suit."

"Thanks," Lauren said, flipping through a stack of twenties.

"Now all you need is one more thing."

"What?"

"Oh, I don't know. Maybe…," Mindy tilted her head to take a closer look at Lauren. "Buy yourself some new earrings. Wild ones. You know, dangly with beads and stuff. To complete the new look."

Lauren smiled at her friend. "Daring earrings, huh?"

"See? Even there. Your smile stands out now like one of those athlete's on a milk commercial. I never noticed it much before. Don't take this the wrong way, but before all anybody noticed was your hair. This was a good move, Lauren."

"It was an accident."

"There's no such thing as an accident when you're a believer, Lauren. You know that."

Lauren gave a little laugh. "As if God really cares about my hair."

"Hey, he happens to know exactly how many hairs you

have on your head! If that's not personal involvement, I don't know what is." Mindy locked her counted cash drawer into its slot and punched some numbers into her computer terminal.

"Well, he has a lot fewer to count now," Lauren said. Usually she agreed with Mindy's view of Scripture, but this was about her hair. She didn't see it as a spiritual issue.

"You know, sometimes," Mindy continued, "we think something terrible is happening to us, and God is saying, 'Hey, relax, will ya? I've got it covered.' My dad used to say that we should never think for one minute that Almighty God is standing in heaven, wringing his hands, and saying, 'Oh dear, oh dear! This wasn't supposed to turn out this way.' God is in control. All day, every day. All the way. You hearin' what I'm sayin'?" Mindy talked at a volume loud enough for several other women to feel included in their conversation.

"You tell her, Preacher Girl," one of the other tellers said.

The women often teased Mindy for her speaking out without hesitation about spiritual matters. It didn't seem to bother Mindy a bit. She was never ashamed of the gospel of Christ.

Lauren used to be bold about her faith when she was in high school. She came from a church that had a strong youth group, and she had read through the Bible before she went to college. Four years at a Christian college had increased her Bible knowledge but mellowed her zeal. Ever since she had been with Jeff she had toned down even more. Jeff's approach to Christianity was to be a good example and let his life naturally speak of his reverence for God. Lauren agreed with Jeff, yet she admired Mindy's spunk. In many

36

ways she was glad to be around Mindy, especially because she was always honest.

When Lauren was leaving work that evening, Mindy ran out the door and caught up with her in the parking lot. The heat of the midsummer's eve surrounded them, luring from the asphalt a pack of pungent, invisible tar snakes. Mindy smoothed back her thick, black hair and focused her dark eyes on Lauren. "Are you nervous?"

"Nervous? Why?"

"What if Jeff doesn't like your hair?"

"Why shouldn't he?" Lauren said, unlocking her car door, eager to get in and turn on the air conditioner.

"It's a big change."

Lauren could feel the pent up heat from the day escaping from her open car door.

Mindy continued. "Moving to New York is a big change, too."

"I know."

Mindy raised her arm to shade her eyes from the evening sun. "You keep reminding yourself that God is in control, all right?"

"I will," Lauren said. "I know he is. Everything will work out fine." Lauren was about to tell Mindy she had decided not to go to New York and to ask Mindy to pray for her as she tried to convince Jeff to give up the idea of New York. Something stopped her — something inside that had been chiding Lauren for days, telling her she wasn't capable of making wise decisions. So she swallowed her insecurities, gave Mindy a hug, and slipped into the car, tugging on her straight skirt.

How does Mindy manage to read my mind like that? I wish I

felt as convinced as she does that everything is going to turn out okay. Maybe Jeff will tell me tonight that he's changed his mind about New York, and I won't have to be the bad guy in this. Maybe another position has opened up here in Nashville. Maybe he'll like my hair…

At exactly six o'clock, Lauren pulled up to the front of The Ambassador. After turning her keys over to the parking attendant, she slipped into the restroom to run some lipstick across her lips. As she pursed her lips together, she checked her eye makeup. It was light; a few twirls of the mascara wand wouldn't hurt. After doing the top lashes, she decided to give a twirl to her lower lashes, which was something she didn't usually do. Stepping back to examine her handiwork, she was surprised to see that Mindy was right. Her eyes did look much larger and much bluer than they ever had before. Some daring earrings would look nice instead of the small pearls she wore. With a quick squirt of perfume and a few picks with her fingers to fluff out her bangs, Lauren held her head high and exited the restroom, ready for Jeff and whatever reaction he might have.

She slipped past the maitre d', who was on the phone, deciding to prowl through the elegant, darkened dining room on her own. It would make her surprise for Jeff that much more fun. Lauren noticed several men glancing up from their meals as she sauntered by, but none of them was Jeff.

A man with large, annoying eyes sat at a back booth and seemed to be watching Lauren's every move. He had slick, dark hair and wore a trim business suit with a deep red tie. She couldn't see the person sitting across from him in the booth because the back of the high seat blocked her view.

She looked away and thought, *If that's a woman sitting with him, she should feel insulted by the way he's gawking at me.*

Lauren stood in one place, her eyes roaming the room for Jeff. The crystal chandeliers cast their soft, glittery light against the rich, white table linen. Their arrows of light shot out in a precarious fashion before being extinguished in the plush maroon upholstery and the ornate Indian rug.

The gaze of the unattractive man at the booth met her glance again. He lifted his glass to her and let his wry smile express his thoughts. His dinner guest then glanced around the corner of the booth and took a good look at Lauren. He imitated the gesture by lifting his glass with a smile before disappearing around the velvet-backed booth.

A pixie-like smile danced on Lauren's lips as she crossed her arms in front of her and began to tap her foot. With her tongue in her cheek, she waited for the second man to do a double take. It only took a moment before he snapped his attention back to Lauren and immediately rose to come greet her. She stood her ground, waiting for him to come to her.

"What are you doing?" Jeff said, reaching her in the middle of the restaurant and speaking in a low growl that didn't match his polite facial expression.

"What am I doing?" Lauren answered playfully. "I'm meeting my fiancé for dinner. What are you doing?"

"Waiting for you. I thought you'd be late. I told Garry you're always late. What are you trying to prove? And what did you do to your hair?"

Lauren had never seen him so emotional in public. "We're having dinner with Garry?" she asked.

"Why didn't you ask me before you cut your hair?" Jeff's eyes scanned her as his expression reflected his disapproval.

"Why didn't you tell me we were having a business dinner?"

Jeff grasped her elbow and led her to their booth, a tight smile pressed across his tensed jaw. "We've been making some decisions," Jeff said between clenched teeth.

"You and Garry?" Lauren said, trying to make Jeff look at her again. He kept looking ahead and stepped up to the table.

"Garry Taft," he said, "I'd like you to meet Lauren Phillips." Then, as almost an afterthought, he added, "My fiancée."

"Very pleased to meet you," Garry said, rising and shaking her hand. He seemed unembarrassed by his earlier flirting. "Forgive me if I appear a bit surprised. Jeffrey said you had long hair."

"I used to," Lauren said politely, settling into the booth next to Jeff. "I just got it cut."

"It's stunning. You're stunning," Garry said. "You didn't tell me you were engaged to such a gorgeous woman, Jeffrey."

Jeff smiled and let out something that sounded like a cross between a huff of disbelief and a nervous laugh.

"Waiter," Garry called as the server in black coattails passed their table, "a bottle of champagne, please." Then turning to Lauren he said, "We have some serious celebrating to do here. Did Jeffrey tell you all about our big plans for him with Burrows, James, and Tompkins? The next time I treat you kids to a night on the town it'll be in New York!" He lifted his glass in a toast to Jeff and then to Lauren.

She turned to Jeff for an explanation. He was looking straight ahead, toasting back to Garry. Lauren knew what that clench in his jaw and his cool demeanor meant. Not to touch him or talk to him. His mind was made up. She knew he had agreed to take the position in New York, with or without her.

Four

Alone in her quiet apartment, Lauren sat curled up on her cabbage rose couch and pulled her cotton robe tight. It was not quite dawn on this somber Saturday morning in July. This was the morning Jeff was leaving for New York. It had been two and a half weeks since the fateful dinner at The Ambassador and the heated discussion that followed at her apartment.

They didn't make coffee. They didn't talk calmly. Jeff accused her of "flipping out" because she cut her hair, and of embarrassing him at dinner by turning down the champagne. He wanted to know what had gotten into her and what had happened to the soft-spoken, predictable woman he had asked to marry him.

Lauren countered, asking what had happened to the easygoing, dependable man who wanted to live in the country. Why was he suddenly drinking so much and saying *ciao* to everyone?

Jeff called her narrow-minded and insecure. She said he was trying to be something he wasn't. He told her she didn't understand. When she replied, "Maybe I could understand if you didn't shut me out," Jeff got up and left, slamming the door behind him. He had done this to her twice before in their relationship. No, three times. Each time she had patiently waited for him to come back, and he had within a few hours.

This time he didn't return. He didn't call. Lauren wavered between convincing herself hope still existed for their relationship and inwardly agreeing with her raw emotions that it was all over between them.

For the next few days Lauren kept her problems to herself. She told Mindy she and Jeff had had a disagreement about New York and were still working it out. Since it was so busy at work, she and Mindy hadn't been able to take their lunch breaks at the same time, which helped Lauren remain detached. To her, it was better to wait and pray than to announce the failure of her engagement. All couples have arguments. Maybe they would pull out of this. It would save a lot of embarrassment later if she kept quiet now.

After three long days of little food and little sleep, Lauren received a call from Jeff at work. She met him at Giovanni's. He apologized. She apologized. She asked if perhaps they should see a pastor or a counselor. He bristled and said he couldn't marry her.

She said nothing as she gave him back the ring. He slipped it into the starched pocket of his white shirt and ordered cappuccinos for them. Lauren sipped hers silently as Jeff cleared his throat and told her about the new leather seat covers in his car, as if the two of them were now officially acquaintances, amiable ex's.

As a final gesture of her love for Jeff, Lauren drew on

every ounce of emotional strength left in her heart and honored him by not crying in public.

She went to work the next morning and pulled Mindy aside to tell her. Mindy cried, but Lauren didn't. She asked Mindy not to make a public scene but to let Lauren tell certain people when she was ready.

By Friday, everyone knew, and they all presented her with a gift before the bank opened. It was wrapped in a small, flat box with a white ribbon. Inside was a note that said, "Here he is: the perfect man. He's sweet, he's silent, and if he gives you any trouble, you can bite off his head." Under the tissue was a big gingerbread man. They all had a good laugh. Lauren was glad to be laughing and not crying.

During the next week, Mindy had bits of advice, some spiritual, some practical, but all compassionate. Lauren found herself praying constantly, not so much asking God why, as asking what she was supposed to do now.

She called Jeff once at work, which he never liked her to do. She asked if she could stop by his place that evening. He said he had plans, apologized, and then said he would try to see her before he left on Saturday.

Now, here it was, Saturday morning, and Jeff hadn't called or stopped by. She had known he wouldn't. Jeff liked clean breaks. He had told her once how he skipped a year-end party at college because he didn't want to have to say good-bye to a bunch of people who would make an emotional scene.

What Lauren had the most difficulty with was trusting herself and her instincts. How could she be so wrong about a man's being the right choice for her?

She and Jeff had met in Shelbyville, a small Tennessee

town where her parents had moved when Lauren went away to college. Her stepdad had this dream of raising walking horses, and Shelbyville was the place to do it. Lauren had come to live with them after she finished college and then had gone from job to job in California, never finding the right position.

Jeff was in Shelbyville, visiting an uncle for the weekend, and met Lauren at a corner gas station. She was filling her car's tank when he stopped and asked directions. She told him to follow her, and she would direct him to the right road. In the process, she got a flat tire, and Jeff helped her to change it. Then he asked for her phone number. They went to the movies the next night, but when she sat down in the darkened theater, the seat gave way on the left side, jarring Lauren and causing their tub of popcorn to fly into the lap of the stranger next to her. That was the first time Jeff had asked, "Do these sorts of mishaps always happen to you?"

Early in their relationship Jeff would laugh with her. Then he took on the role of her protector. He helped her acquire her present job so she could move to Nashville and be close to him. Their dating relationship moved forward. Everyone, including Lauren's parents, were delighted to see her at a steady job. The only problem was Lauren didn't like numbers or money or anything about banking.

When she moved to Nashville, her plan had been to use her English degree as the foundation for a teaching credential. It meant she had to take a few more upper division courses, and those would have to be night classes. But that was okay. She at least had a goal, finally, and planned to work on obtaining her teaching credential as soon as they were married.

Now all those plans had vanished into emptiness. She had no plans.

Lauren reached over the top of the couch to the drawstring hanging from the window and gave it a pull, raising the pleated shade to let in the morning. The view from her window was peaceful. A patch of pine trees ran along the back side of the apartment complex. The summer morning sky began to warm, as if the pilot light of the sun had been lit and any moment now burners all across the heavens would catch the flame and set the sky ablaze.

Suddenly she heard heavy footsteps on the outside stairs leading to her front door. Lauren held her breath, staring at the closed door. The door knocker was lifted and tapped firmly two times.

Lauren slid off the couch, her heart pounding. She straightened her robe and quickly ran her fingers through her hair. She knew she looked haggard and grabbed a tissue, trying to wipe off the dark mascara rings under her eyes.

The knocker sounded again, twice. Lauren cleared her throat. "Coming!" She tried to sound composed. Her hand clutched the brass knob, and she let out a huge breath before opening the door. A pleasant smile was on her face as she prepared to greet Jeff.

But the man at her door in the early morning haze was not Jeff. This man was scruffy looking, unshaven, with brown hair parted crooked on the side and hanging almost longer in the back than Lauren's. He held a battered box in his arms and wore a gray T-shirt and jeans.

"Oh, good. You're up," he said.

"Bradley," Lauren whispered in disbelief. "What are you doing here?"

46

"Since when does a guy need a written invitation to visit his sister?" The athletic young man walked in and asked, "Where do you want me to put this?"

"Put what?"

"Your computer."

"My computer?"

"Yeah, I brought you a computer." He waited for a response, and when he didn't get one, he said, "And now you're supposed to say, 'Thanks Rad! You're a doll.'"

"Thanks, Rad. You're a dork. What are you doing here?"

"Visiting you."

"You mean to tell me you drove all the way here from California without even calling to tell me you were coming?"

He gingerly placed the box on the kitchen table. "I knew you would be home. Mom told me that donkey dumped you. Thought you would like a little cheering up. So, ta-da!" He spread his arms and gave her a cheesy grin. "Here I am!"

"Jeff didn't dump me. It was mutually agreed that we discontinue our relationship."

"Oh yeah, right," Brad said, opening the refrigerator door. "You've rehearsed that one a few times. This isn't a job interview, Wren. It's me, Rad. Remember? I know it's been a few months..." He took the milk out of the fridge and sniffed it before drinking out of the carton.

"Try years, Radley. When did you grow your hair out?"

"A while ago," he said, sliding the milk carton back into the refrigerator. He turned and looked at Lauren. "Did you do something to yourself? You look different."

Lauren pulled a strand of hair out to its full length. "Could it be my hair, which used to hang to my waist?"

"That must be it. You look different," Brad said, looking

her over. "Actually, you look pretty good for someone who just got dogged."

"I didn't get dogged."

"Oh, that's right. What was it? 'Mutual disagreement' or whatever? You got dogged. Totally. What I can't figure out is why would anyone dump you? You're the best, Wren." He poked his head deeper into the refrigerator. "Don't you have anything to eat around here?"

"Get out of there. I'll make some breakfast." Lauren set to work making a blowout breakfast for the two of them. She hadn't eaten much in days, and her vegetable bin was full of ingredients for an omelet. Brad found a box of pancake mix and went to work alongside her, making Mickey Mouse pancakes.

It brought back lots of memories for Lauren. The two of them had always been close. Brad was only thirteen months younger than Lauren, and their mom had referred to them as slow twins. Their father left before Brad was born and never came back. In all her twenty-four years, Lauren had only wondered a few times about her father: what he was like, why he left, if he was still alive.

When she was fifteen she wrote a composition for English about a girl who was abandoned by her father when she was young and grew up to be a nurse. Years later the nurse was treating a terminally ill patient who was homeless and had lost his memory. The doctors wanted to let the welfare patient die, but the nurse took pity on him and did all she could to keep him alive. She cared for him tenderly, as if he were an infant. In the end he died anyway. When the nurse went through his few belongings, she found a picture of herself as a baby and a newspaper clipping of her marriage announcement. The man was her father, and even though he wasn't capable of being a responsible parent, he must have never stopped loving her.

Lauren won a city-wide contest with that essay. It was the closest she had ever come to exploring her feelings about her birth father. Brad never knew him. Their mother married Stanford James Phillips, a Canadian with a strong temperament. He brought order to their family when Lauren was just beginning kindergarten, and he was a generous provider for them. Lauren and Bradley never doubted that Stan loved them or that he was crazy, head-over-heels in love with their mother. For all intents and purposes, he was their father.

Brad considered him to be his only father. Lauren never had a problem calling him "Dad" or taking his name when he adopted them. But somehow, through the years, she and Brad had bonded in a way she never had with her mother, nor Brad with Stan. Lauren and Brad were in their own circle. And it was a small circle with only enough room for the two of them.

The first thing Brad did after stuffing himself with every last pancake and Lauren's omelet was to set up the computer and printer he had brought her. He told her they were about to enter the Web. They would now be able to e-mail each other daily at a minimal cost. Brad yammered on about how much it bothered him that Lauren hadn't called to tell him about the broken engagement.

"What if Mom hadn't called me?" Brad challenged. "When were you planning to tell me? Christmas?"

"I wouldn't have told Mom if she hadn't called," Lauren said. Earlier that year their mom and Stan had moved back to Stan's hometown of Victoria, British Columbia, after giving up on the five or so years of trying to start the walking horse business in Shelbyville. "Are you going to computerize Mom and Dad, too?" Lauren teased, clearing the breakfast dishes.

"I've thought about it," Brad said. "But I only had one spare computer, and I decided you needed it more than they did. I got it from my roommate. He upgraded and traded me this dinosaur unit for my mountain bike and a bunch of CDs."

"I still can't believe you drove all the way here. In what? How long did it take you?"

"I drove my truck. Did you know I bought a truck?" Brad said, ducking under Lauren's narrow desk and plugging in the computer. "It only took a couple of days. Nice drive. Okay," he said, kicking off his floppy loafers.

"Your feet smell," Lauren said.

Brad ignored her and flipped a switch on the side of the monitor. "We have lift off." He pulled the chair closer, and his fingers flew over the keyboard.

"Rad?"

"Hmmm?" His eyes were glued on the screen.

"Nothing."

"Okay," he answered.

Lauren wanted to pour out her heart and ask her brother all the questions that had been chasing around in her brain that morning. Questions such as: What should I do now? Why should I stay in Nashville? Where would I move? Certainly not back to Shelbyville. And she had no desire to move in with her parents in Canada. Brad was wrapped up with his college life and friends in southern California. She couldn't slip into his life. At least in Nashville she had a steady job and some good friends like Mindy. And there was the reason she had told her parents she was moving to Nashville in the first place. She had told them it wasn't completely because of Jeff. It was also because so many colleges were available. She could finish up her teaching credential. Perhaps that was the answer, as obvious as it seemed.

Something Jeff said during their last meal at Giovanni's loomed over her, something about his not wanting to hold her back from realizing her potential. Yet there seemed to be a twist to his words. The message she had read between the lines was that she was the one holding him back. And he had decided to go about his life without her.

A stab of familiar pain accompanied the thought. Abandonment. Rejection. Failure. The hurt dug down so deep within her heart all she knew to do was to shut it out. And she knew how to do that quite well.

Brad worked feverishly, making a few phone calls, tapping away at the keyboard, and plugging in the well-used printer. Lauren cleaned up the kitchen and thought about how useful this computer was going to be. She wouldn't have to use her ancient word processor to type her papers if, or should she say when, she went back to school.

"*Voila!*" Brad suddenly announced. "Get ready to ride the info highway, Wren, baby! And be sure to fasten your seat belt, because this highway ain't paved."

Five

Okay, Lauren, come here and let your little bro teach you a thing or two," Brad said.

Lauren stood behind him at the computer and watched the screen suddenly go blank.

"You were saying?"

"Okay, okay. So I don't have all the bugs worked out yet. Give me a minute or two." He turned and glared at her with mock annoyance. "Don't you have anything better to do than stand over my shoulder all day nagging me? Go get a life, you pathetic woman!"

For some reason, his teasing hit a nerve, and Lauren started to feel the room closing in on her. In a small voice she answered, "I don't have a life." The glass of milk in her hand began to quiver.

"I was only kidding," Brad said, trying to read her expression. "It's not your fault that jerk dumped you."

A numb feeling began to invade Lauren's brain.

"You're better off without him."

"Yeah," Lauren said aimlessly. She imagined Jeff boarding

the airplane right now, leaving her forever.

"Hey, you don't look so good," Brad said.

"No," Lauren said, a haze of insecurity settling over her. "I don't suppose I do." A gurgle bubbled up in her throat. A swallowing of tears and an attempt at laughter combined into one indefinable sound.

"I think you're starting to lose it, Wren. Maybe you should go to bed. Take a little nap. Get your head clear." Brad stood up and cautiously approached her. "Come on, lady," he teased. "Put the glass of milk down nice and easy, and nobody gets hurt."

Lauren fell into a crazy laughter mixed with tears and put down her glass of milk.

"That's right," Brad coaxed. "Come with me. Back to bed. A little nap is in store for you, missy."

"But I'm not tired," Lauren protested as Brad led her to her room.

"Right. You've barely eaten or slept for weeks, and you don't think your body needs any refueling. You're cruel, Wren; heartless and cruel to treat your frail flesh like that. Take a rest. Go ahead. Lie down."

Lauren complied.

Brad pulled the covers over his sister, tucking her in nice and snug. "That's it. Close your eyes." His deep voice lowered to a whisper, "Go to sleep. Shhh."

Lauren's spasming chest settled into a normal breathing pattern. She suddenly felt tired. Very tired. Brad's strong hand rested on her cheek for a moment, and then she was asleep.

When Lauren woke, it was dusk. The room seemed small. Forcing her eyes open all the way, an invisible weight pressed against her forehead. A moment later she remembered what day it was. Then it all came back, rushing at her with unhappy urgency.

He's gone. Jeff is out of my life forever.

The covers stuck to her legs, and she kicked them off. Her queen-size bed was made up in white cotton sheets and frosted with a coverlet she loved. She had found it in a catalog several months ago and saved up the $119.99 to buy it. It was called "Tulips Jacquard" in the catalog and was a white-on-white, loomed quilted coverlet with a tulip design embroidered around the scalloped border. The ad said it was imported from Portugal. When it arrived, Lauren was sure it was the nicest thing she had ever owned.

Taking several deep breaths, Lauren gazed around her room, waiting for her eyes to adjust.

Only two pictures were on the walls. One was a Monet-style watercolor in blues and soft golds with tiny, muted red tulips in the background. The other was a Norman Rockwell poster of a young man in a suit and a young woman wearing a yellow dress standing on her tiptoes as she signed a marriage license before the justice of the peace. Lauren had bought it at a poster shop right before her first year of college.

Her roommate, Teri, had said that every time she looked at it, she wished she were the woman in yellow. Lauren felt the same way. The picture opened up many conversations for the two of them as to what kind of man they wanted to marry and what they thought marriage would be like.

Now all Lauren's dreams of marriage were shattered. She expected to feel a swell of emotions that would draw the tears back to her eyes. Instead, she felt a strange sense of calm. For the first time in weeks she felt as if she was going to be okay. She wasn't going to lose her mind after all.

What did this new peacefulness mean? Was Jeff going to come back?

Propping herself up on her elbow, she listened carefully. A male voice spoke in the next room. She eased her feet out from under the covers and walked quietly to the door, opening it a crack and peering into the dining area.

"Make that an extra large with the works," Brad was saying into the phone. "What's that? No, I don't have any coupons. Okay. Thanks. Bye."

"What time is it?" Lauren asked, walking out and squinting in the light.

"Dinner time, sleeping beauty. Are you hungry? I took the liberty of cleaning out the refrigerator for lunch, so dinner is on me. It'll be here in thirty minutes."

"You are too kind," Lauren said, bending in a mock bow.

"Anything for your majesty," Brad said.

"So what have you been doing all day, besides eating everything in my kitchen that isn't plugged in?"

"Bringing you into the twenty-first century. Come here. Sit down. I want to show you this." Brad was still in his gray T-shirt and jeans, barefooted. His hair was now flipped behind his ears, and the stubble on his chin was edging more toward a beard than a five-o'clock shadow, showing he had lost track of time. She felt unexplainably proud of her brother. He looked like a hippie and smelled awfully ripe. In the few short hours she had slept, he had trashed her kitchen and strewn empty cookie boxes, smashed soda cans, and two plastic trays from microwave meals around her small desk. Still, she was proud of the slob and glad he had come. Brad was all heart when and where it really counted.

Lauren pulled up a chair and said, "You need a shower. You seriously need a shower."

"Okay, okay. As soon as I show you how to do this." Brad began to walk her through all the steps to turn on her new computer, connect with the Internet, prepare and send mail, and enter a chat room. As they entered their second chat room on the computer, the doorbell rang.

"I've got it," Brad said, hopping up and pulling his wallet from his back pocket. He paid for the pizza as Lauren, fascinated, watched messages being typed in before her eyes, knowing they were coming from varying parts of the world. Everyone had an opinion, a comment, or a question. And for every action there was an equal and opposite reaction. Amazing. She had heard about this cyberspace of modern communication but to see it suddenly flashing across a computer screen in her little apartment was astounding.

"So what do you and I do to talk to each other?" she asked.

Brad stuffed a slice of steaming pizza in his mouth and mumbled, "You want some?"

"No. I'll wait till it cools off. Plates are in the cupboard, Rad."

"No problem. Yeow! This stuff is hot! How could it still be hot? Do you have any more sodas?"

"There's some in the fridge."

"Not anymore. I'll settle for water. Unless you have an espresso maker."

Lauren looked at her brother and shook her head. "What are you: a yuppie or a hippie? Make up your mind."

He shrugged and took a hit of water right out of the

faucet. Then, joining her, he said, "What were you asking about e-mail?"

"This isn't e-mail, is it?" Lauren asked

"No, e-mail is private. Like a letter. No one else can read your e-mail unless you want them to. You and I will be able to send messages back and forth all the time for literally pennies. See, I send the letter to your local holding tank. This mailbox icon here on your screen will let you know if you have any mail waiting, and then you can open it and read it anytime you want, right off the screen."

"That's pretty amazing," Lauren said. She quickly handed him a napkin from the counter just before a pepperoni slipped off his pizza and landed on the keyboard.

"Good eyes," Brad said. "Melted cheese is the worst to try to clean out of the keyboard." He licked his fingers and sat down next to Lauren.

"I'm serious about that shower suggestion," Lauren said.

"Okay, okay. Just watch this. We're going to jump in here." Brad typed in:

ANY GL'S IN THE ROOM TONIGHT?

"GL? What's that?" Lauren asked.

"It's an underground code a couple of guys in my Bible study group got going. It stands for God Lovers. If you say Christian anymore you get all kinds of responses, not necessarily from Christians, but from everyone else who thinks he knows what Christians are all about. Look, there's a response."

Across the screen came the message:

GL — YES. KC. E-ME AT...,

and then came a string of letters and numbers.

"What kind of code is that?" Lauren asked.

"That's his address."

"How do you know what it means?"

"Easy. It's someone who goes by the initials KC. He's a God Lover, and that's his mailbox number. He's inviting correspondence. Let's write him."

"What are you going to say?" Lauren asked.

"Watch." Brad tapped in:

HEY, KC. HOW'S IT GOING? I'M VISITING MY SISTER, WHO'S
RECOVERING FROM A BROKEN HEART. HOW ABOUT YOU?
EVER HAD ONE OF THOSE?

He signed it "Rad & Wren" and sent it to KC with Lauren's new electronic address on it. "That's your code now," Brad explained to Lauren. "You needed a name for the Net. You don't mind using Wren, do you?"

"Like it matters. You already used it. Did you send that letter?"

"Yep. If KC writes back it'll come to your address. It appears I've just found you a pen pal." Brad looked pleased with himself and celebrated by going for another piece of pizza.

"Why did you have to go and broadcast my private life to some stranger?"

"Since when did you care about your privacy?" Brad challenged. "You used to be an open book to anyone and everyone, particularly grocery clerks and UPS delivery men."

Lauren got up, pulled a plate from the kitchen cupboard, and went looking for something to drink. The fridge was almost empty.

"You weren't kidding, you chow hound. You're buying groceries tomorrow."

"You're avoiding my question. Can we thank Mr. Jeff for

this new, closed-tighter-than-a-vault version of Lauren Michele Phillips?"

"Can we just drop it, Bradley Dane Phillips?"

He knew better than to push. Lauren realized his comment contained an element of truth. She had changed during the time she was with Jeff.

"Hey, look!" Brad said. "You received a letter. From KC, no doubt."

"Who else did you expect?"

"Cool. Let's see what he has to say."

"How do you know it's a man?"

"I don't. I just assumed. Read it between the lines."

"How can you read between the lines when it was only one line? And a short one at that."

"Listen to this," Brad said and started to read:

HEY, RAD & WREN, NICE TO MEET YOU, BROTHER—AND SISTER. SORRY TO HEAR ABOUT THE BROKEN HEART. I HAVEN'T HAD THE SAME EXPERIENCE, BUT WOULDN'T WISH THAT ON ANYONE. THERE'S ALWAYS A REASON, YOU KNOW. I UNDERSTAND BROKEN HEARTS CAN ACTUALLY BE A GOOD THING. AT LEAST GOD SAYS THOSE ARE THE KIND OF HEARTS HE'S NEAR TO. (I THINK THAT'S ABOUT CHAPTER 34 — PSALMS.) SO DO YOU KNOW DOUG? HE'S THE ONE WHO TURNED ME ONTO THE GL CODE. PEACE, KC

"Are you going to write him back?" Lauren asked.

"No," Brad said, punching in some numbers. "You are. There. I saved his address. See, this is your address book. You pull it down like this. That's my e-mail number, and there's KC's. Two pen pals. Now you're on your own. I'm going jogging."

"Jogging? You just stuffed yourself with pizza."

"You're right." Brad stretched both arms over his head and said, "I'll unload my car instead. I hate to take a shower unless I'm good and sweaty."

"Believe me," Lauren said, "you're good and sweaty."

Brad seemed to notice his odor for the first time. "Maybe you're right. Which way to the shower?"

When Brad emerged twenty minutes later in clean shorts and T-shirt, looking and smelling much nicer, Lauren teased him and said, "Oh, yes, I see the resemblance now. It was hard to be sure you were really my brother under all that dirt."

"Did you send a message back to KC?" he asked, checking out the blank computer screen.

"No. I shut down the computer. Thought it wouldn't hurt if I tried to save a little electricity." Lauren was in the kitchen, unloading the dishwasher.

"What? KC wasn't interesting enough for you? You want me to find you another pen pal?"

"I don't need any pen pals."

Brad entered the kitchen and put his arm around his sister's shoulders, pulling her close. "Yes, you do," he said. "You need me. And you need to write me and talk to me and use me as your underpaid psychiatric advisor and parole officer."

Lauren laughed. It felt good.

"And my first bit of free advice is this: You are alive. Your whole life is still before you. More terrible things will happen to you. Wonderful things will happen, too. Don't run from life, Wren. Embrace it."

She turned to Brad and wrapped her arms around him. "I love you."

"You better," he said, giving her a squeeze and a kiss on the forehead. "Now what do you say we go out for some ice cream?"

$\mathscr{S}ix$

The weekend passed wonderfully warm and encouraging for Lauren as she let Brad cheer her up and entertain her. They went to church, jogged, and ate massive amounts of Chinese food. And because Brad had paid for the groceries, Lauren almost willingly watched three Star Trek videos with him as they sat surrounded by a boatload of junk food.

Monday after work Lauren returned to her apartment to pick up Brad. The two of them then met Mindy and her husband, Leon, at the park where Leon had already initiated a pickup game of basketball.

"I'm in," Brad said, raising his arms to get the guys' attention. Someone shot him the ball, and he was transformed into Captain Dribble.

"That's your brother?" Mindy said from her solitary spot at the picnic table. "You didn't tell me your brother was so cute."

"No, but if you ask him, I'm sure he'll tell you how cute he is." Lauren sat down and dropped her bag of food on the table. "I picked up some chicken and potato salad. What did you bring?"

"The whole refrigerator." Mindy motioned to the big ice chest on the ground at the end of the picnic table. "I didn't want to take the time to figure out what to bring so I scooped everything into there." She perched herself on top of the picnic table, and facing Lauren, asked, "So, are you recovering?"

"I don't know," Lauren said with a sigh. "I'm fine now because Brad's been working hard at keeping me happy. But I can't help feeling as if I've made a horrible mistake. Maybe I should have gone to New York with Jeff. I haven't been making good decisions lately. Ever since I decided to get my hair cut —"

"No," Mindy jumped in, shaking her head. "Don't you see? Cutting your hair was your way of symbolically breaking with the past. You felt trapped by Jeff, and you knew this would push him away."

"I don't think so, Min."

"Sure. Didn't you ever see that movie where the guy works at a bakery, and his arm is chopped off in one of the machines? And then — who is that actress with the long hair? Well, anyway, she tells him he felt like a caged animal because of his engagement so he cut off his arm on purpose to scare away the woman. The woman he's engaged to, that is, not the woman he's going to end up with. But he doesn't know that yet."

Lauren smiled. "I think I missed that one. If it didn't have a Vulcan in it, we didn't watch it this weekend."

"Oh, it's a great movie. Very romantic, with a happy ending. And your life will have a happy ending, too."

"Do you have the gift of prophecy, and you never told me?" Lauren teased.

62

A saucy smile graced Mindy's lips as she said, "There's always that possibility."

Six weeks later Mindy made another prediction about Lauren's life. They were locking away their cash drawers in the vault at the end of a hot Friday afternoon in August. Mindy asked Lauren what her plans were for the weekend.

"I need to finish the book I'm reading for my class and write a paper. It's due Monday." Lauren had enrolled in summer school the week after Jeff left. She had checked out the local colleges and found that to earn her teaching credential all she needed was three more English literature courses and one unit of physical education. She had done her student teaching during her junior year of college when she had considered being a teacher. The experience at the public school had been grueling, and she had switched her major to English literature her senior year. Now, with the goal of teaching at a small-town school, Lauren felt motivated to finish what she needed and move on with her life. Going back to school also helped to fill the gap in her social life with studies and a Monday night class.

"Are you still reading that book about those two poets who fell in love through their letters?" Mindy asked.

"Yes, the Brownings." Lauren followed Mindy to the desk of the operations manager, Marie, where they turned in their paper work for the day and were signed out. Marie had been in a good mood ever since her fortieth birthday a week ago, when she had become engaged. It had made for a lot of talk around the office.

"I can't believe I balanced today," Mindy said. "That twenty-seven cents was about to drive me to the loony bin." She grabbed her purse, and Lauren picked up hers. After a round of "good nights," Mindy suggested they take the elevator down to the lunch room to grab a cold soda before venturing out of the air-conditioned building and into the heat.

"Did I tell you," Lauren said as the elevator door shut on the two of them, "that she was thirty-nine when their romance began?"

"Really?"

"Yes, I remember because she was six years older than Robert, and she had tuberculosis."

Mindy stopped in her tracks and placed her hands on her hips. "Get outta' town. I never heard that."

Lauren nodded. "The doctors all thought she was going to die. After a year and a half of writing to each other every day, they eloped, left England, settled in Italy, and at forty-three years old, she had a baby."

"Who are you talking about?" Mindy stood blocking the elevator door with both hands on her hips.

"Elizabeth and Robert."

"Who?"

"Robert and Elizabeth Browning. You know, the poets from the book I'm reading for class. 'How do I love thee? Let me count the ways…'"

The elevator door opened, and they stepped into the vacant lunch room. "He wrote that? I thought that was Shakespeare."

"No, she wrote it. She didn't show it to Robert for several years. Then one morning in Italy, after breakfast, he was looking out the window, and she came up behind him and stuck a packet of papers into his coat pocket. She told him to read them and tear them up if he didn't like them. Can you imagine? Then she left him to read the sonnet alone. She was quite shy. It's a beautiful sonnet. So romantic."

"You're the one who's so romantic," Mindy said, fishing for change for the Coke machine. "I thought you were talking about Marie."

"Marie?" Lauren questioned.

"You know, Marie, our supervisor," Mindy said. "I thought you were talking about real people."

"I am talking about real people," Lauren protested.

"I mean people who live in this time zone. Not somebody buried a hundred years ago in England. Do you have an extra quarter?"

"Italy," Lauren said, handing Mindy a quarter. "Elizabeth is buried in Florence. Robert is buried in England. At Westminster Abbey, to be exact. But he always said his heart was buried in Florence. He outlived her by twenty-eight years and carried her little gold ring on his watch chain." Lauren let out a contented sigh.

Mindy's can rumbled from the belly of the Coke machine, and she stepped aside to let Lauren drop in her quarters. Lauren was staring at the ceiling.

"Hello?" Mindy said, waving her hand in front of Lauren's starry eyes. "You're starting to spook me. Would you mind staying in the here and now, at least as long as you're around me? I mean, I don't mind you telling me about your class and your papers, but when you start talking about these dead people as if they're your friends, well..."

Lauren let her quarters slip into the machine and pressed her fingertips on the selection button. "That's what's so amazing. They do seem real to me. Their personalities and their passions. Why aren't people like that today? Do you know what I mean? Whatever happened to nobility and honor and cherishing another person's feelings? Did I tell you she gave him a lock of her hair and wrote a poem about it being the last strand her dead mother kissed?"

Mindy looked at her with raised eyebrows. "And your point is…"

"Oh, never mind." Lauren headed for the elevator.

"No, no, go on. I didn't mean to shut you down," Mindy said.

Lauren gathered her thoughts as they waited for the door to open. "I guess I'm discovering that I'm very much a romantic at heart. It didn't come out much with Jeff. He was so straight and practical all the time."

"I happen to remember something about flowers Jeff brought you all the time. Flowers are not exactly straight and practical."

"Jeff only brought them because I hinted how much I liked flowers. It wasn't his idea. Don't you see? He brought me flowers as a response to my idea. It wasn't something he did out of a symbolic passion." They entered the elevator, and Lauren pressed the cold soda can against her cheek. In a low voice she said, "What I want is not an obligatory bouquet, but one red rose on my pillowcase. Or a gardenia tied in a pink ribbon on my doorstep with a note that says, 'You are the fragrance in my day.'"

Mindy burst out laughing. "Dream on, girlfriend! And while you're there, dream a good one for me." The door opened, and they exited the building into the humid heat of the summer night. "A happily ever after, that's what you want."

Lauren smiled. "It could happen."

"I know it could," Mindy agreed as they waved good-bye

over the tops of the cars. "And it will for you; you just wait and see. If anybody deserves for it to happen to her, it's you, Miss Romance!"

Lauren slid into the car and cranked on the air conditioning. The CD automatically started up a mellow jazz number, and she drove to her quiet apartment with a smile still on her face, congratulating herself on how far she had come since her breakup with Jeff nearly two months ago. She had cried only that one time in the apartment with Brad. Jeff had been pushed far from her thoughts. She was ready to move on.

That evening Lauren finished reading her book and started on her paper. Five pages into the project, her computer's cursor froze. She tried and tried to get it to move. Nothing worked. Lauren grabbed the phone and called Brad in California. All she got was his voice mail.

Slipping down on her hands and knees, Lauren crawled under the desk and checked all the electrical cords Brad had connected. When she unplugged one of the cords and then stuck it back in the socket, her computer sounded a tone, indicating it had started back up.

"Good," she said, crawling out from under the desk. "Who needs a brainy brother?" After one look at the screen, she took back her words. Her paper was gone. Lauren started to open files, clicking on anything that would respond. It was hopeless. Her five pages had vanished.

"Thanks a lot, you hunk of junk!" she shouted at the unyielding screen. Lauren tried again to call Brad and left a more desperate message on his voice mail, pleading for him to phone her immediately. She decided to send him an e-mail. They had been writing to each other about twice a week ever since Brad had brought her the computer. He was right about it being a good idea. She hadn't corresponded anymore with KC, although the thought had intrigued her many times. There didn't seem to be anything to say.

Her letter to Brad was to the point:

RAD,

HELP! I JUST LOST MY PAPER ON THE BROWNINGS. HOW DO I GET IT BACK?

WREN

She wasn't paying attention when she sent the letter. The instant her fingers were off the keys, Lauren realized she had zapped the letter to KC instead of Brad. She had been meaning to delete KC's number since she had never used it. KC hadn't written her either, so she saw no point in keeping the number. Yet there it was, and she had just sent Rad's message to him.

"You are such a klutz!" Lauren knew she couldn't cancel the letter. It had already taken off into cyberspace, and she knew of no way to "beam" it back home to her computer. She considered writing a note to KC explaining her mistake. However, if she let it go, he might not even notice it. At least she could still send it to Brad, and she did.

Pushing back her chair from the narrow desk, thoroughly frustrated, Lauren decided to let the paper go until tomorrow. She was not in the mood to start all over, especially if Brad might have some ideas on how to pull her hard work out of the jaws of the electronic monster.

It was 9:35. Bed sounded good; bed and her copy of

Elizabeth's *Sonnets from the Portuguese*. Once Lauren was ready for bed and settled under her crisp, cool white sheets, she opened the book at random and read:

First time he kissed me, he but only kissed
The fingers of the hand wherewith I write;
And ever since, it grew more clean and white,
Slow to world-greetings, quick with its "Oh, list,"
When the angels speak. A ring of amethyst
I could not wear here, plainer to my sight,
Than that first kiss…

There was more, but Lauren was content with only that portion to nibble on for awhile. The thought of a man's first kiss being simply on her hands, or better still, as with Elizabeth, the fingers she used to write all those letters to her true love…it was such a romantic notion.

Without planning it, Lauren's thoughts filled with Jeff and one evening they had spent together in the spring walking around Radnor Lake when all the dogwoods were at their peak. They had sat together under a wide, pink dogwood umbrella, and in the quiet of that outdoor cathedral, Jeff had run his fingers through her long hair and told her she was his "silver lining." He said he needed her optimism, almost as if positive thoughts didn't come to him naturally so he needed Lauren to generate them for him. They had kissed and cuddled and didn't mind the gentle spring rain as it misted their clothes with its earth-nourishing gift. All that mattered to her at the time was that they were together and that Jeff loved her and wanted to marry her.

She had caught a cold afterwards. Perhaps it had been a sign. No matter. That was past. Her emotions refused to connect with her memory, and she felt no anxiety or remorse.

Now Lauren knew what she wanted and what she needed: someone who would not only draw from her spirit but would also give back to her and replenish her emotionally, spiritually, mentally, and even physically. Someone who would kiss her fingers. Did such a man exist?

Closing her eyes and giving in to the sandbags weighing down her eyelids, Lauren snapped off the light and drifted into sweet slumber.

She didn't attempt her paper again until Saturday morning and was dearly hoping she wouldn't have to start from the beginning and reconstruct her whole paper. Fixing herself a glass of iced tea, Lauren turned on the computer and connected with the on-line service to see if she had any mail. Two letters awaited her, one from Brad and one from KC. She read Brad's first:

WREN,

ONE QUESTION: DID YOU SAVE AS YOU WERE GOING? IF YOU DID, CALL ME. WE MIGHT BE ABLE TO RESURRECT IT. OTHERWISE, EVEN A POWER SURGE CAN BLIP YOUR UNSAVED PIECES FROM HERE TO KINGDOM COME. HEY, SOUNDS LIKE A GOOD SPIRITUAL ANALOGY CAN BE DRAWN FROM THIS—BEING SAVED AND THEN RESURRECTED. DID I TELL YOU I STARTED TO TEACH A SUNDAY SCHOOL CLASS OF BARBARIAN SEVENTH-GRADE BOYS? I NEVER BELCHED IN PUBLIC WHEN I WAS THIRTEEN, DID I?

RAD

After muttering to herself about how she should have known better and should have saved the paper as she was working on it, Lauren punched in a response to Brad:

RAD,

I DIDN'T SAVE IT AS I WAS WORKING ON IT. I KNOW, I KNOW. AND THE ANSWER TO YOUR BELCHING QUESTION IS, OH YES, YOU DID. MUST GO. I HAVE A HUGE PAPER TO WRITE.

LOVE, WREN.

She sent the letter and was about to sign off when she remembered the letter from KC. To her surprise, her heart began to pound a little faster as she read his words:

WREN,

BY NOW YOU'VE CERTAINLY REALIZED YOU SENT ME THE WRONG LETTER. IT WAS NICE TO HEAR FROM YOU ANYWAY. DID YOU SOLVE YOUR COMPUTER PROBLEM? BY ANY CHANCE WERE YOU REFERRING TO ROBERT BROWNING? I DID A PAPER ON HIM IN COLLEGE. ONLY GOT A B+, BUT I DID LOTS OF RESEARCH ON THE GUY. I EVEN HAVE SEVERAL BOOKS ON HIM STORED IN A BOX SOMEWHERE. IF I CAN BE OF ANY ASSISTANCE, PLEASE HOLLER. DID YOU KNOW THAT ROBERT TAUGHT HIMSELF THE BASICS OF HOMEOPATHIC MEDICINE? HE GAVE UP TEA, COFFEE, AND WINE AND TOOK A TINY DOSE OF STRYCHNINE EVERY DAY. I WOULDN'T HAVE A PROBLEM GIVING UP COFFEE OR WINE, BUT FORGET THE STRYCHNINE. I DO LOVE TEA. IRISH BREAKFAST. WITH CREAM AND SUGAR. ADDICTING. HOPE ALL GOES WELL WITH YOUR PAPER. IS IT FOR A CLASS?"

PEACE, KC

If she had thought about it, Lauren probably never would have responded to this stranger's note. As it was, she started to write a long letter back, opening herself up to KC. She was thrilled to know another person who had "met" one of her Victorian friends. Her fingers flew over the keyboard as she composed line after line, telling KC all about her class on Victorian literature and her favorite facts about Robert and Elizabeth. With a tap on the "send" button, her letter was mailed. Then she went to work on her paper, the words coming effortlessly.

Lauren received an A on the paper and an A in the class, which so excited her that she e-mailed KC to tell him, even though he hadn't yet responded to her long letter earlier that week.

She didn't hear from him at all until Labor Day weekend. His words were worth the wait:

WREN,

GOOD FOR YOU! WHAT NEXT? RENAISSANCE LITERATURE? I'M ASSUMING YOU'RE AN ENGLISH LIT MAJOR. I MAJORED IN JOURNALISM, SO I ONLY GOT IN ON A FEW OF THOSE ENLIGHTENING CLASSES LIKE VICTORIAN LITERATURE. I HAVE AN INTERESTING ASSIGNMENT COMING UP IN A FEW DAYS. I'M GOING TO EGYPT. IT'LL BE GOOD TO GET OUT OF THIS ROOM CLUTTERED WITH PAPER AND TAKE IN SOME FRESH AIR. I HAVEN'T BEEN ANYWHERE SINCE MY BROTHER'S WEDDING IN JUNE. I'VE NEVER BEEN TO EGYPT. HAVE YOU? OH, BY THE WAY, I FOUND ONE OF MY BROWNING BOOKS. THIS ONE IS ALL ABOUT THE HOUSE THEY LIVED IN IN FLORENCE: CASA GUIDI. THEY WERE THERE FOR FOURTEEN YEARS. DID YOU KNOW THAT ROBERT REGULARLY

STALKED THE FLEA MARKETS FOR FURNITURE AND ENDED UP WITH SOME VALUABLE PIECES FOR ONLY A FEW POUNDS? MY KIND OF GUY.

CONGRATS AGAIN ON THE A. KEEP UP THE GOOD WORK.

PEACE, KC

Surprised at the way her heart was swelling, Lauren realized KC's praise meant more to her than the encouragement she received from Mindy and Brad put together. Here was someone who shared her interest on a much deeper level. Someone who "knew" her Victorian friends and yet remained mysterious. Someone who liked to find bargains at flea markets and was going to Egypt.

Lauren leaned back in her desk chair and read the letter again as it scrolled down the computer screen. KC said he hadn't been anywhere since his brother's wedding in June. She and Jeff had broken up in June. Even though she hadn't left Nashville since then, she felt as if she had been places. Through her summer reading, she had been to Italy with Elizabeth and back to England with Robert after Elizabeth's death. Lauren had grown this summer. Not just because of the class, but because of the new independence the breakup of her engagement had forced on her.

She started to write a letter back to KC:

KC,

THANKS FOR THE ENCOURAGEMENT. I'M GLAD TO KNOW THE NAME OF THE BROWNING'S HOME IN FLORENCE. IF I EVER GO TO ITALY, THAT'S THE FIRST PLACE I'LL VISIT. HAVE YOU BEEN TO ITALY?

YOUR JOB SOUNDS INTERESTING. EGYPT—HOW EXOTIC! I
HOPE ALL GOES WELL FOR YOU.

AS YOU GUESSED, YES, I'M AN ENGLISH LIT MAJOR. I HAVE
ONE MORE CLASS THIS FALL AND THEN PLAN TO FINISH UP
MY TEACHING CREDENTIAL—NOT THAT I KNOW WHAT I'LL
DO WITH IT. BY THE WAY, I'M A BARGAIN HUNTER, TOO.

Lauren paused and thought back on her summer. Nearly
every weekend she had gone "treasure hunting" to garage
sales and flea markets. Some weeks she would find only a
lace doily or a cheese grater, and her total purchases after an
hour of poking around would add up to a quarter. One week
she had found an antique dresser with a beveled mirror. The
mirror was cracked, and two of the knobs were missing on
the drawers. Within two weeks she had a fabulously restored
antique dresser in her room, replacing the old pine chest of
drawers.

She decided to share a bit of her bargain hunting with
KC:

MY BEST BUY OF THE SUMMER WAS AN ANTIQUE OAK
DRESSER. IT'S LOOKING MUCH HAPPIER NOW THAN IT WAS
WHEN I FOUND IT.

She paused again, thinking now of a recent e-mail from
Brad. She had told him about some of the changes that were
taking place in her life, and Brad's response had been, "It
sounds to me as if someone has given you permission to find
yourself this summer. Good. Enjoy the thrill of the hunt!"
She hadn't understood his comment at the time. Now it
made sense. She was free to do the things she enjoyed without having to worry about trying to make someone else

happy. A treasure hunt of her heart. Some days the amount of growth would equal little more than a twenty-five-cent doily. Other days she could see places inside her being fixed and restored like the antique dresser.

I JUST REALIZED THAT I'M A LOT LIKE MY DRESSER. I'M HAPPIER NOW THAN I WAS AT THE BEGINNING OF THE SUMMER. I WENT THROUGH A PAINFUL BREAKUP AND DIDN'T THINK I'D EVER FEEL PEACEFUL AGAIN. ACTUALLY, WHAT GOD HAS DONE IS GIVE ME A WHOLE NEW KIND OF PEACE. GOD IS SO INCREDIBLE, ISN'T HE? WELL, I PROBABLY SHOULDN'T BE POURING MY HEART OUT TO YOU LIKE THIS. YOU HAVE A TRIP TO PACK FOR! BE SURE TO TAKE YOUR SUNGLASSES. I HEAR THE GLARE OFF THE PYRAMIDS IS PRETTY BLINDING.

JOY! WREN

Lauren clicked the "send" button and glanced at the clock on her kitchen wall. It was 12:20. She had no idea she had been absorbed with her letter to KC for more than an hour. The Labor Day picnic for the bank employees had officially started twenty minutes ago. Lauren's taco salad was already made, waiting in the refrigerator, and the bag of accompanying tortilla chips sat on the counter.

A tug-of-war began inside of Lauren. She wanted to go to the picnic, but part of her wanted to stay right here, in front of her computer for the rest of the day, waiting for a reply from KC and then responding back to him. She hoped her letter hadn't sounded too personal. The words had come so naturally as she wrote them.

Lauren laced up her tennis shoes, packed her salad and chips, and headed for the front door. As she left her apartment and stepped lightly down the stairs, she wondered about KC. What did he look like? Was he old? Young? Where did he live? Was he married? She didn't think he was. Why would he correspond so freely with a woman who was obviously young and single if he were married? Was he possibly interested in her? How could he be after a few simple letters?

Cranking the key in the ignition, Lauren reminded herself that Robert and Elizabeth had met through only a few simple letters. She remembered from her paper the first line of the first letter Robert wrote her: "I love your verses with all my heart, dear Miss Barrett."

"With all my heart," Lauren repeated aloud as she came to a stop sign. The romance fairies had begun their work, sprinkling their dream dust all over her thoughts until reality became quite clouded. All Lauren could think of was that someday, somehow, somewhere, a man would say to her, "I love your letters with all my heart, dear Miss Phillips."

Eight

Centennial Park brimmed to nearly overflowing with picnickers as Lauren drove through the parking lot a second time looking for a spot. None of the carefully lined up cars were budging. She gave up and drove three blocks away before finding a spot. As Lauren hiked through the muggy September afternoon with her salad in her arms, she wondered if all the lettuce would turn to mush before she found the group from the bank.

Her coworkers were already lined up to eat, so Lauren quickly slipped her salad onto the end of the table and removed the foil covering it. Ripping open the bag of tortilla chips with her teeth, she sprinkled them on top and then wedged the bag next to the bowl for anyone who wanted more. It was a delicious salad, one she had learned to make from Teri, her college roommate.

Lauren said hi to a few of the people standing around her and was about to make her way to the end of the line when someone called her name. "Lauren? Lauren Phillips? It is Lauren, isn't it?"

She turned to see the large, annoying eyes of the man who had bought Jeff and her champagne and dinner at The Ambassador.

"Garry Taft," he said, stretching out his hand to shake hers. Then looking around he added, "Where's Jeff? Did he come down for the weekend?"

Everyone was looking at Lauren, or so she felt. She toned her answer a few notches lower than Garry's question and said, "Jeff isn't here. We aren't together anymore."

Garry instantly turned into Mr. Sympathy. His brown eyes seemed to change from annoying to weepy puppy-dog eyes. "Oh, Lauren, I didn't know. Jeff never said anything. I assumed you were in New York. If I'd known, I would have called you. Are you doing all right?"

"I'm fine, thank you." Lauren nervously pinched the tablecloth. She glanced around to see if Mindy might be near and could help her out of this awkward situation. She didn't notice that Garry was reaching for her arm. He tenderly grasped it and pulled it toward himself in a gesture of concern. Lauren was still pinching the vinyl tablecloth, and as Garry tugged on her arm, the cloth came with it, upsetting the two salad bowls on the end of the table.

In one spastic motion, a bowl of potato salad and Lauren's bowl of taco salad toppled over onto her bare legs and tennis shoes. "Look out!" Garry cried, after the incident was over. "I mean, are you okay?"

A glob of green guacamole clung to her right knee. Her shoes were covered with sour cream, wilting lettuce, and crumpled tortilla chips.

"Entirely my fault," Garry said, stooping to help by running his hand down her leg, smearing the guacamole.

"That's okay," Lauren said, brushing his hand off her leg. "I'll find some napkins for you."

A crowd had gathered around her at the end of the line, their plates heaped with food. Lauren tried to move out of the way. An older woman offered her a napkin, and one of the men from the loan department handed her a bottle of water to use. Garry returned with a heap of napkins and more apologies.

She could hear Jeff's voice echoing in her head. *"These things seem to happen to you, Lauren."*

"I'm fine," she said to Garry and the others standing around. She scooped the ruined salad, along with the wad of potato salad on the ground, into the broken teakwood salad bowl and carried it to the nearest trash can. It upset her that she had spent all that time and expense on her deluxe salad and now it was ruined. And her bowl was broken. A memory flashed through her mind of Jeff saying the bowl was cheaply made when she bought it. She didn't want to think about Jeff. And she didn't want to spend another second around Garry.

"Hey, you!" Mindy called from a few yards away. She and Leon were walking across the grass toward Lauren. Mindy waved and tugged on Leon's arm, urging him to move faster. He held a big salad bowl in his hands.

"Can you believe this crowd?" Mindy asked from behind her sunglasses. "We had to park five blocks away. Are we too late? Is everything gone?"

"No, there's plenty —" Before she could finish she heard Garry's voice behind her.

"Here's a plate for you, Lauren. Are you ready to get in line with me?"

Mindy pulled down her sunglasses and gave Garry a close examination over the top of the rims. Then she turned to Lauren for an explanation.

Without even turning around to look at Garry, Lauren said, "Garry, these are my friends Mindy and Leon. This is Garry, ah..."

"Taft," he said, filling in for her memory lapse. He stretched out a hand to shake with Leon and then Mindy.

"Jeff used to work with Garry," Lauren said to Mindy.

Mindy's lips formed a silent, "Oh."

"You arrived at the right time with that salad," Garry said, eyeing the covered bowl in Leon's arm. "I hope it's potato salad!" Garry was about an inch shorter than Lauren and that made him more than a foot shorter than Leon.

"It's taco salad," Mindy said. "I made it from your recipe, Lauren. Remember that one you made when Leon and I came over last spring?"

"Oh, yeah," Lauren said dryly. "I know just the salad."

"What do you say we all grab ourselves some food before it's gone?" Garry suggested, leading the way back to the table as the three of them followed their unchosen leader.

Mindy set her salad bowl on the newly opened spot at the end of the table and said, "Look at this, Leon. Someone else brought tortilla chips. I told you it didn't matter that I forgot them."

Lauren bit the inside of her mouth. More and more she was liking the idea of going home and writing another letter to KC. She had never told Mindy about KC, partly because the e-mail system she had going with her brother and with KC never had come up as a topic of conversation. The deeper reason, though, was that she didn't want Mindy or anyone else to give her any negative feedback about KC. She didn't want to be cautioned, teased, or counseled. All she wanted was for her easy, private, and often soothing communication with this unknown man to continue unhindered by anyone or anything.

"Over here, Lauren." Garry flagged her to the front of the line with the paper plate in his hand. Leon, Mindy, and Lauren joined him as Lauren said to Mindy between clenched teeth, "Don't you dare leave me alone with him. Not even for one second. Do you understand?"

"Got it," Mindy said.

Garry handed each of them plates. Mindy used hers as a fan. "So, Garry," she said, "what brings you to this gathering of money-changers?"

"Didn't you know? I'm your adman. You know the billboard with the puppies for sale at the ATM machine? That was my brainstorm." Garry reached for a burger. Instead of putting it on his plate, he put it on Lauren's. With a smile he said, "Ladies first. That's what I always say."

Lauren was furious. The puppies had been her idea, which she had told Jeff, and he had presented it to his committee. The ad idea occurred to her when she saw a boy stand by the front door of the bank last Christmas with a box of kittens for sale. After two hours of hard peddling, he had come into her teller window and asked if she could give him a fresh twenty-dollar bill for his pocketful of kitten profit.

She didn't mind Jeff using her idea or getting the credit for it. At least at the time she hadn't. It had made her feel a part of his world. But for Garry to say it was his idea was something else. If her salad hadn't already been dumped, she would have dumped it over his head.

When they sat down, Lauren turned her back to Garry and purposefully didn't eat the hamburger he had put on her plate. She didn't enter into the conversation but kept her mind whirling, trying to think of how to get rid of Garry. Fortunately Mindy had been socializing and formulating a plan at the same time.

"Isn't that Justin McKinley over by the volleyball court?" Mindy said, flipping down her sunglasses to have a better look. "I've been looking for him. Will you all excuse me?"

Lauren flashed her a "don't leave me" look. Too late. Mindy was up and gone. At least Leon had been carrying the conversation with Garry. They were going through all the businesses in town with which Anchor Advertising had an account. Garry flexed his intellectual muscles for Leon by reciting ad slogans for each business.

Mindy came back right away, announcing that Justin needed one more player for his team—a woman—and Lauren was his choice. Lauren didn't mind a bit. She loved volleyball. It would also allow her to keep her distance from the marketing maniac.

"Great," she said, hopping up. Then, as firmly as she could, she added, "Good-bye, Garry," hoping it would sound like the dismissal she intended it to be.

"*Ciao*, baby," he said, winking one of his cow eyes at her. "You go knock 'em dead!"

Lauren gave Mindy's arm a little squeeze of thanks and jogged over to the volleyball court. Her legs felt sticky from the guacamole. White and green specks still clung to her shoe laces.

"Hi," Lauren said, a bit breathless and perhaps a bit too eagerly. "Mindy said you needed another player."

Charming, southern Justin McKinley put his arm around Lauren's shoulders and said, "You stick with me, darlin'. I'll keep that barracuda away from you."

Mindy, you weren't supposed to tell him about Garry!

Justin was one of the leaders of the career group Lauren had begun to attend at church after she and Jeff broke up.

"What barracuda?" Lauren said coyly. She liked Justin from the first day she had visited the group. He had an easy-going manner, a great sense of humor, was a natural leader, and looked like a movie star: tall, tanned, and athletic. He was someone she wouldn't mind getting to know better. The chances of that had improved considerably when, two weeks ago, Justin had showed up at the bank. He had just been hired to work for a radio station that had its office on the fifth floor of their building.

"You mean to say you're not interested in my protection services?"

"I don't know what you're talking about," Lauren said with a smile in her voice. "I came over here to play some serious volleyball."

"That's what I want to hear," Justin said. He left his arm looped around her shoulder and told her to stick with him, and they would rotate in.

Lauren peeked over her shoulder. Yes, Garry was watching her.

"You know," Justin said, tilting his head slightly toward hers, still watching the game, "I would kiss your lips right here and now and give him a good show, but I don't kiss on first dates."

"This isn't a first date," Lauren answered playfully.

"Then we'll have to go on one. What do you say? This

Friday night? You and me, and we'll leave the barracuda at home."

"How do I know you're not a barracuda in disguise?" Lauren said.

"I'm not a barracuda. I'm a vegetarian. Now will you go out with me? I know a great place for salads."

"As long as it's not taco salad," Lauren muttered.

"What's that? Was that your answer, and I missed it?"

They still hadn't made eye contact. His arm was comfortably around her shoulder, and they both were watching their team as it made another point. Justin was up next to rotate in.

"So, who's winning?" asked a voice right between the two of them. It was, of course, Garry.

Justin dropped his arm and gave the outgoing player a high five as he jogged in to take his place. Before the server could call the score, Justin waved his hands over his head and yelled, "Wait! Hold up!"

He had everyone's attention, especially Lauren's because his dark green eyes were focused directly on her. Everyone else followed his line of sight.

"Did you say something, Miss Phillips?" he asked politely. "I believe we were waiting for an answer from you regarding Mr. McKinley's question about a date this Friday night."

Lauren felt her cheeks turn crimson. Garry, startled, stood next to her. This was a huge step, reactivating her social life in such a public way. Clearly Garry would get the message to bug off. She pressed her lips into a smile and nodded her head.

"I'll take that as a yes," Justin said in his best radio announcer voice. Turning to the rest of the team he said,

"Thank you." And then to the other team, "Thank you. I couldn't fully concentrate until she had given me a straight answer. You know how it is with women. They like to keep you guessing."

Nine

The week sped by, and Lauren felt young and free-spirited, looking forward to her date Friday with Justin. Garry had eventually disappeared at the picnic, and Lauren and Justin's team had won the volleyball tournament. More than once Justin had praised her game skills. She loved volleyball. It was the only sport she had played much.

Justin had stopped by her teller window every day that week since the picnic. Tuesday he cashed a check for twenty dollars. Wednesday he asked for a roll of quarters, saying it was time he did some laundry. Thursday he stopped by her window to give her a candy bar, stating that the machine down in the lunchroom had flipped out and given him two Snickers for the price of one.

Now it was Friday afternoon, and Lauren's stomach curled into a knot. She hadn't seen Justin all day. Her window faced the main entrance and the elevator, and she had kept glancing over in that direction, expecting to catch a glimpse of him at any time. She replayed the way he had flirted with her at the picnic and how he had been unashamed to let everyone in the volleyball pit know that he had asked her out. It seemed like high school all over again, and Lauren couldn't help but wonder if she weren't regressing by being so caught up with the excitement of going out with Justin. Dating Jeff had been so much more staid and "mature."

At lunch that afternoon Mindy had asked her what she was going to wear, and Lauren had confessed she had five different outfits laid out on her bed waiting for her to get home and decide.

"This is a big deal to you, isn't it?" Mindy had said.

"I suppose." The lunchroom was crowded, and Lauren didn't want anyone to hear what she was saying, especially someone like Justin, who had just as much access to this lunchroom as anyone else who worked in the building. "It's my first date since Jeff," Lauren said softly.

"The way you've been moony-faced all week, I'd think it was your first date ever." Mindy leaned closer. "Don't get me wrong. I like Justin. I don't much like the idea of this being such a huge event in your life. It gives him the potential of breaking your heart."

"That's already been done," Lauren said.

"All the more reason for you to approach bachelor number two with caution. Do you get what I mean?"

"You're suggesting I might be on the rebound?"

"Bingo!" Mindy said.

"It's been more than two months. I'm over Jeff. He's ancient history. Do you see me crying over him any more?"

"I didn't see you ever cry over him." Mindy made one of her puckered faces, which meant "you don't get it yet."

"Don't look at me like that," Lauren said. "I'm telling you,

I'm over Jeff. Have I even once mentioned him to you in the past three or four weeks?"

"That's what makes me nervous. You were in love an awfully long time to be out of love so easily."

"You know what, Mindy?" Now Lauren leaned closer. "I'm not even sure Jeff and I were actually in love."

"You were."

"I don't know."

"I know," Mindy said firmly. "Love comes in all shapes, sizes, and styles. Yours may not have turned into an ever-after love, but it was love, all right."

"I don't think it was love at all."

"See? This is why you worry me. You stuff those feelings in any deeper, and you're going to need to buy a bigger size of jeans. You're not over Jeff. Not completely. You bounced back way too fast."

"Oh, yes, I am over him," Lauren said, standing up, ready to go back to work. "And tonight I'll prove it. Call me tomorrow if you want the full report."

"You know I do. What time should I call?" Mindy rose and they headed for the bathroom.

"Anytime."

Just as they turned the corner to enter the women's restroom, Justin came hustling out of the men's restroom. It was an awkward moment.

"Hey, I was about to come find you," Justin said. "Is 6:30 still okay?"

"Sure, that's fine," Lauren said. Mindy lingered by her side.

"How's it going, Mindy?" Before Mindy could answer, Justin snapped his fingers. "I know what I was meaning to ask you, Lauren. What's your apartment number? I didn't see it on the map you drew me."

"F-52. It's toward the back."

"Great," he said, breaking into his earnest grin. "See you at 6:30 then."

Lauren lifted her hand to wave good-bye. He was already on his way up the stairs. She glanced at Mindy, who had a questioning look on her face.

"What?" Lauren asked.

"Do you have any idea what a fine looking man he is?"

"Yes, I do, and may that be a lesson to you."

"A lesson to me?"

"Yes. Stop being so negative about my first date with him. Everything is going to be great."

Lauren was still telling herself that at 6:25 as she tore around her apartment trying to find her other earring. She had bought a pair of dangling earrings with blue beads at a flea market in July, and now one seemed to be missing. She had decided on jeans and a simple white T-shirt. It was basic and could be easily dressed up, like with the dangling earrings. Now where was that other one?

While on her hands and knees looking under the sofa, Lauren remembered taking an earring off a few days ago as she talked on the phone. Scanning the kitchen counter, her eyes caught on a tiny blue bead inside the box of Kleenex tissue next to the phone. She grabbed the earring and slipped it on just as an energetic knock sounded at the front door.

"Hi, Justin. Come on in."

"Hey, nice place you have here," Justin said. He wore jeans, cowboy boots, and a Hard Rock Cafe T-shirt. His sun-bleached hair was slicked back, and he smelled like lemons and wood smoke mixed together. Fresh and woodsy at the same time.

"It's kind of a mess," Lauren said. "I couldn't find this earring, and I nearly tore the place apart looking for it."

"Looks like you found it," he said, checking her ears and then admiring her in a full scan. "You look real nice."

"Thanks. Let me grab a jacket, and I'll be ready to go."

"It's still hot as blazes out there. I don't think you'll need one."

"You think so?" She couldn't think straight. Her linen blazer was part of her ensemble. It made her look much more put together than the simple white T-shirt. "Maybe I'll grab it just in case."

"Fine with me," Justin said as she disappeared into the bedroom. "What on-line service are you with?" he called after her.

Lauren returned with the blazer on, sleeves pushed up, and a thin strapped little leather purse slung over her shoulder. "What did you ask?"

"I asked about your computer. Are you on-line?"

"I am, but I have to admit I don't know any of the technical terms. My brother is the computer geek, or brain, whichever you prefer. He brought me the computer and hooked me up so we could keep in contact with each other. It's worked out nicely. We e-mail each other a couple of times a week. The computer has been great, too, for homework. Did I tell you I'm going to school?"

"No. Why don't you tell me all about it on the way. I made reservations for 6:45."

After checking to make sure her front door was locked, Lauren followed Justin down the stairs. A bright red sports car waited for them in the first uncovered spot.

"That's yours?"

"Yes, ma'am. I do hope you don't mind a little wind in your hair."

"How fun," Lauren said, hopping in. "This is adorable! How long have you had it?"

"'Adorable,'" Justin repeated. "Mabel here has been called a lot of names. You're the first one to call her adorable. I'm sure she'll be your friend for life because of it. I got her from my grandpappy in Kentucky. He bought her thirty years ago and hardly ever took her out. My granny said Mabel here was his mid-life crisis. As long as she was in the barn, Granny didn't have to worry about his taking off with other women."

Justin revved up the engine. "My grandpappy passed away three years ago, and he left me good ol' Mabel. This little sweetheart has cost me more than two cars twice her size would have." He patted the dashboard and said in a smooth voice, "Don't take any of that personally, girl."

Lauren could feel herself beginning to relax. By the time they arrived at Clementine's, which was a bustling restaurant, she felt the thrill of being with Justin starting all over again, as it had at the volleyball game at the Labor Day picnic. Several people at the restaurant greeted Justin by name. He waved and smiled a big, friendly greeting to all of them as he and Lauren wove through the loud bar area into the restaurant.

She had never been to Clementine's. It looked like a fun, earthy sort of place from the outside with its wooden flower boxes and green shutters. Inside it was equally charming. The tables were all different sizes and shapes, made from a wide variety of woods. Bunches of wild flowers hung from pegs on the wall. At the end of each table a live, potted plant was embedded in the wood. Some of the plants grew a full three to four feet above the table, creating a cozy camouflage from the rest of the tables. The room was light and airy like a mountain cabin. Lauren liked it.

"I always wanted to try this place," Lauren said as they sat down and picked up the menus in front of them. "I even suggested it to Jeff a few times, but he never wanted to try anything new." The minute the words were out, she stopped herself. What was she doing talking about Jeff?

"Was Jeff your last boyfriend?" Justin asked. If he felt threatened by her mentioning Jeff, he didn't sound like it.

Lauren wished she hadn't brought him up. "Actually, we were engaged."

"Really?" Justin appeared interested. "How long ago did you break up?"

"June."

"Is he still in town?"

"No. He went to New York. Listen, Justin," she laid down her menu, "we don't have to talk about Jeff. I'd much rather talk about you."

Justin held up a hand to silence her. "Hey, doesn't bother me a bit. The guy had his chance. He obviously blew it, and you're fair game."

"I don't know if I'd call myself 'fair game.'"

"Sorry. Old country-boy talk. What I'm trying to say is, I don't mind your talking about whatever you want to talk about. Might help you to get some of your feelings out in the open."

"I don't know," Lauren said, pulling back from the tender

93

subject. She shifted her focus to the menu and asked, "So what do you recommend?"

"All their salads are great," Justin said.

Lauren decided on the Sunshine Salad with romaine lettuce, mandarin oranges, grated carrots, and sunflower seeds. As the waiter placed a basket of warm, twelve-grain rolls before them with a dish of butter, Lauren attempted to launch into another topic of conversation with Justin. "It's my turn to host the newcomers luncheon this Sunday. Do you want to come? I think only two other people have signed up."

"Sure." He leaned across the table and said, "If you don't mind my asking, why did you and — what was his name, Jeff?"

"Yes."

"Why did you and Jeff break up? If I'm getting too personal, you can slap me, and I'll hush up."

Lauren smiled and said, "No, that's okay." She didn't really feel it was okay, but she didn't know how to gracefully slip out of the question. "We broke up because Jeff was offered a position in New York, and, well, he pretty much made the decision to accept it with or without me. I guess he assumed I'd follow him."

"And you're not a follower," Justin suggested.

"I have been. I followed Jeff here to Nashville."

"Well, I'm glad you stayed," Justin said, letting a Wiley Coyote grin take over his face. "I'm not much of a New York person, either."

"I've only been there a few times," Lauren said as their salads arrived. "But I don't think I could have lived in New York. Not for very long, at least. I prefer small towns. Jeff said he would like to live in the country, but he didn't really mean it, I don't think."

Justin nodded and silently encouraged her to continue.

And continue she did. During their entire meal Lauren talked about Jeff: How different he was from her; how blind she had been to the imbalances of their relationship; how she now realized Jeff had held her in a sort of emotional bondage.

By the time they finished their meal, Lauren felt yucky. All this pouring out of her heart and evaluating their relationship had made her feel foolish and blind to have ever gone with Jeff in the first place. Justin didn't say anything that made her feel that way; she drew her own conclusions while listening to herself talk. A deep, sinking feeling clung to her as they left the restaurant.

Justin suggested they drive around town with the top down. Even with the wind in their hair and the cool of the evening to blow away the depressing thoughts, Lauren still felt burdened, weighed down with the uncomfortableness of her own words and the direction the evening had taken.

"You know what, Justin?" she said as he pulled up in front of her apartment. "I really enjoyed having dinner with you, but I feel as if I put a gloomy shadow over the whole time with all my talk about Jeff. This isn't how I wanted the evening to go."

"Doesn't matter," Justin said calmly. She realized his smile was now her silver lining. "First dates are always supposed to be awkward. Maybe this gave you a chance to get some things out in the open, and that's good."

"I appreciate your patience and your listening ear." Lauren gave his strong arm a gentle squeeze. "Do you want to come in for coffee?"

"Thanks, but I need to be at work early in the morning. I'm filling in for a guy who's on vacation. Tune into the station tomorrow morning, and I'll keep you company from five to ten." He said the last line as if he had practiced it more than once for an advertisement.

"Thanks again for a really nice night," Lauren said, reaching for the car door handle.

"Whoa, let me get that for you. Can't let all these manners my mom taught me go to waste." He hopped out of the driver's side and came around the front of the car to open her door. Justin reached for her hand to help her out and then promptly let go of it as they walked up the stairs to her front door.

Lauren pulled her key out of her purse and unlocked the door, "Well, I'll see you Sunday."

"Sunday," he confirmed, giving her an amiable smile. "Good night." He bounded down the stairs.

Lauren entered the silent house with tears clouding her eyes. "You are such a jerk!" she muttered to herself. "How could you have been so clueless? You ruined the entire night." She slunk into the kitchen, preparing to make coffee out of habit. The ceramic coffee canister was empty, and the bags of coffee beans she usually tucked in the freezer weren't there. She tried to remember the last time she had made coffee. It had been weeks. The only time she used to drink it was with Jeff after their dates.

With a heavy sigh, she snapped off the kitchen light and headed for the living room couch where she sat in the dark. Outside her window, Mr. Toad rippled his consistent chorus. He never seemed to give up. Perhaps Sunday things would be different. Justin said he would come for lunch. If first dates were supposed to be awkward, then they were right on schedule.

Promising herself not to mention Jeff, Lauren made a midnight wish that she would have a second chance with Justin on Sunday.

Ten

I hope you know this isn't helping me a bit," Lauren said as she and Mindy stood in line to pay for a pair of jeans Mindy was buying at Dillard's. "How many times do you want to hear that you were right and I was wrong? It's just that Justin was so open and understanding and had such a kind listening ear —"

"That you decided to talk that ear right off," Mindy finished for her. They stepped up to the register, and Mindy handed the clerk her jeans and her credit card.

"It wasn't like that," Lauren said. "I didn't decide anything. It simply turned out the way it turned out, and I realize now I could have redirected the conversation. The whole focus of the evening would have been different."

"Actually, I'm glad you went through this enlightening experience," Mindy said, leaning over to sign the sales slip. "The thing I don't think is so great is the way you've convinced yourself that Jeff was a total bum. You were once in love with the guy, remember?"

"No, I wasn't."

"Lauren, Lauren, Lauren," Mindy said shaking her head. She took the bag from the salesperson and said, "Thanks, you have a good day, too." Then, turning back to Lauren, she said, "As long as I've known you, Lauren, you've needed happy endings. Right now, things with Jeff are left on an unhappy note. Why don't you call him and have a nice, civil conversation and resolve this relationship on a happy note?"

"How is that possible?"

"It's possible." Mindy led the way to the elevator. "With God, everything is possible."

Several other shoppers had joined them and were waiting for the elevator.

"You need to hear and understand the truth," Mindy said, her bluntness moving to the fore. "Truth hurts and truth heals, if you let it. It's the truth that sets you free. You won't spend the rest of your life with a big 'if' hanging over you." She used her hands to indicate a big bubble over her head and opened her eyes wide as she said it.

"A big 'if'?" Lauren repeated quietly, hoping Mindy would take the hint and lower her voice.

"*If* only I had done this, or *if* he hadn't said that. You could spend the rest of your life trying to come up with conclusions to make yourself feel comfortable. And none of them might be the truth. Come on, you grew up going to Sunday school; you know all this. God is in control."

The elevator doors opened, letting out a mom with her stroller. Mindy, Lauren, and four other people entered. As the door shut, Mindy stepped onto her invisible soapbox and began to preach to her captive audience.

"Christianity is nothing less than a complete surrender to God. You know that. Every day, in every situation."

Lauren was conscious of the stares of the people around them.

"It means seeking him first and always, and choosing to trust him even when it's so hard it hurts. It's a life of complete abandonment to the Lover of our souls." Mindy's arms spread wide in dramatic gestures as her voice echoed off the elevator's enclosed walls. "It means going against the flow of everything that seems natural and deliberately choosing God."

The elevator door opened. Lauren was aware of the staring eyes following them as they exited and headed for the parking lot.

"The bottom line," Mindy said, pushing open the glass door, "is that you have a problem with trust."

"I do not," Lauren snapped.

"Oh, yes you do! You have to learn to trust God, to believe that he's in control."

"I trust God, all right," Lauren said with a tease in her voice. "It's his children I find flaky."

Mindy shook her head and unlocked her car door. "I happen to be one of his children. Are you saying I'm flaky?"

"Okay, wacky then," Lauren said, getting in and giving Mindy a playful punch in the arm. "I'm only kidding you! Don't look so serious."

Lauren didn't mind it when Mindy was fired up. Sometimes she even agreed with her. It's just that there was a time to receive a sermon and a time to lighten up.

"You think I'm kidding you about trusting God, but I'm not."

They were silent for a few minutes before Mindy said, "This is what you do. You go home, call Jeff, have a nice heart-to-heart conversation, and then tomorrow you'll be free when Justin comes for lunch. You'll be able to center your attention on him."

"You make it sound so easy."

"Why shouldn't it be?"

"I don't know. Nothing has been lately."

"Now, there you go again. You can't spend the rest of your life acting as if you are Little Miss Victim."

"You're right. You're right, you're right, you're right!" Lauren said, holding up her hands. "Can we drop this topic for awhile?"

"Okay," Mindy returned with a surprised tone in her voice. "It was only a suggestion. Do you want to stop at the Waffle House for something to eat?"

"No, I'd rather get right home."

"No problem. I'll pick up Leon and take him out to eat with me. That man can eat anything, anytime, anywhere." Mindy chattered happily about her husband all the way to Lauren's apartment.

Lauren couldn't believe how exhausted she felt. What she needed were a few encouraging words from her brother. She turned on her computer and checked her mail. Nothing new from Brad or KC. She pulled up KC's last letter, curious if he had specified when he would return from Egypt. No dates were mentioned. The world of KC and his intriguing letters seemed like one universe while this mess with Justin and Jeff seemed like a parallel reality. The dimension with KC was dreamy and unspoiled. Reality was, well…reality.

With one last glance at KC's most recent letter, Lauren pulled down a "reply" file and tapped out a message to Brad:

RAD, WELL, I DID IT. I FINALLY WENT ON A DATE. IT WAS A MAJOR DISASTER. I SPENT THE WHOLE NIGHT TALKING

ABOUT JEFF AND WHY WE WERE SO WRONG FOR EACH OTHER. JUSTIN WAS MORE POLITE THAN ANY MAN SHOULD HAVE BEEN IN THAT POSITION. MINDY SAYS I SHOULD CALL JEFF AND TRY TO MAKE PEACE. WHAT DO YOU THINK? JUSTIN IS COMING OVER TOMORROW AFTER CHURCH. I'M HOSTING A LUNCH GET-TOGETHER FOR NEW PEOPLE IN OUR CAREER GROUP. MAYBE I'LL BE ABLE TO HAVE A SECOND CHANCE WITH HIM. I THINK YOU WOULD LIKE JUSTIN. HE'S NOTHING LIKE JEFF. AND TO HIS CREDIT, HE'S A MANIAC ON THE VOLLEYBALL COURT. PLEASE RUSH ALL YOUR MUCH NEEDED ADVICE TO YOUR LOVELORN SIS.

WREN

Feeling rather proud of herself for having some sense of humor left, Lauren zapped off the e-mail to Brad and began to close the file. Suddenly she froze. The disaster had happened again. She accidentally had sent the letter to KC instead of Brad.

"Lauren, get a brain, will you?! I can't believe you are such a dork!" This time she decided to send an immediate explanation to KC:

KC,

YES, IT'S THE MAD E-MAIL BOMBER, SENDING MORE ACCIDENTAL MAIL TO YOU. WILL YOU DO ME A HUGE FAVOR AND DISREGARD THE LETTER YOU JUST RECEIVED FROM ME? BETTER YET, COULD YOU NOT EVEN READ IT? OR BETTER YET, COULD YOU FORGET YOU EVER MET ME? NOT THAT WE HAVE MET . . . WELL, I THINK I'VE FLUBBED UP ENOUGH FOR ONE LIFETIME. I DO HOPE YOU HAD A TERRIFIC TIME IN EGYPT. AS YOU MIGHT GATHER, THINGS HAVE BEEN PRETTY BORING AROUND HERE FOR ME. SO, IN CASE WE

Allowing herself only a few minutes to think about it,
Lauren sent off the second letter to KC and then sent the
original to Brad. She reached for a notepad and wrote herself
a warning that said, "Check automatic 'send' addresses
before sending e-mail" and taped it to the top of her computer
screen.

Justin noticed her note the next day during her luncheon
and asked her over the background music on the stereo,
"Are you having a problem with your e-mail?"

"I was, but I think I have it figured out." She smiled, hoping that none of her insecurities leaked through. Justin was
the only one who had arrived so far. She was thankful he
had come. He hadn't changed his mind since Friday, and it
gave her hope that a second date might be in their future. In
the five minutes Justin had been there, he had selected the
music while Lauren pulled together the deli buffet of cold
cuts, sandwich fixings, and salad.

"Do you need some help in there?" Justin asked. The
music was awfully loud. Lauren figured he must be used to
it at that level from the radio station. She was more comfortable with subtle background music.

"Sure, you can help me. Would you grab that big basket
on top of the refrigerator and put all these kaiser rolls in it?"

"Sure thing." Justin effortlessly reached for the basket. He
looked over the buffet she was assembling on the kitchen
counter. "A do-it-yourself deli. That's a good idea. I still don't
know how many people are coming. We called everyone on
the list who had come to any of our meetings during the last

month. By the way, did you talk to the woman who came this morning? What was her name? Annie?"

"I think it's Amy. Yes, I gave her directions. She said she was coming. Did you hear her say she grew up in Brazil? Her parents were missionaries there. She just moved to the States two weeks ago and is living with her aunt and uncle."

"Brazil?" Justin looked impressed. "I imagine she'll have some interesting stories to tell."

Lauren couldn't help but wonder if he subconsciously meant that Amy's stories about life in Brazil would be more interesting than Lauren's long ramblings about Jeff. Amy was a few years younger and seemed fairly naive about life. In some ways Amy reminded Lauren of herself. She had long, wavy blond hair; a deep, rich tan; and a lyrical laugh. Her face was tender and lovely. At least that's how Lauren used to see herself. Now, with her hair so short, she thought of herself as older. More seasoned after the engagement. Amy hadn't lost that innocent look in her eyes yet.

There was a knock at the door. Lauren brushed off her hands on her skirt and slipped past Justin to open the door. The last person she expected to see stood there.

"Garry?"

"Hello, Lauren. I was in the neighborhood and thought I'd stop by."

"How did you know where I lived?" The alarm she felt sounded in her voice.

"You're in the book."

"Who is it?" Justin asked, rounding the corner to check on their guest. He seemed as surprised as Lauren.

"I didn't realize you had company," Garry said. "Nice to see you...Justin, is it?"

"How you doing?" Justin politely extended a hand.

Just then Amy appeared at the bottom of the stairs. "Hello," she called out cheerfully. "I take it this is the right place."

"This is it," Justin said.

"Looks as if you have a party going on here," Garry said. "I'm not imposing, am I?"

Amy apparently didn't hear what Garry said to Justin and Lauren. She came up behind him and said, "Hi, I'm Amy."

"Garry Taft," he said, returning her friendly greeting.

An uncomfortable moment of silence canopied the four of them on the tight landing in front of Lauren's apartment door. Inside, the music blared away happily. None of them said anything as they self-consciously grinned at each other.

Just then the phone rang.

"Excuse me," Lauren said. She hurried to grab the phone and had to cover her ear to hear over the music. "Hello?" Over her shoulder she was aware that people had entered her apartment. She turned to see Justin and Amy, and behind them came Garry with a look of victory glimmering in his oversized eyes.

The person on the other end hung up. Lauren returned to the kitchen and tried to think straight. Amy asked if she could do anything to help. Lauren said she thought everything was about ready, and then there was another knock at the door. Two guys from the group stood there with cheesy grins on their thin, bespeckled faces. Somehow she had the feeling these two were a team who had made it their goal to visit every singles' group in town. Lauren's church happened to be next on their list.

She forced a gracious welcome and showed them into the

living room where Justin stood by the stereo, chatting away with Amy.

Someone knocked on the door. Lauren swung it open and a woman who was older than Lauren by a few years greeted her with, "Your map was terrible. I've been driving around this apartment complex for half an hour."

Justin turned up the music another notch, and Garry called out from the kitchen loud enough for everyone to hear, "Hey, Lauren, don't you have any beer around this place?"

Eleven

A t three o'clock that Sunday afternoon, Lauren saw her guests to the door, all except Garry. He had already left, and Lauren felt both horrible and relieved about it. When he had asked about the beer, she had answered with a firm "No!" and had given him a pained expression that accurately reflected all the exasperation she felt at the moment. He obviously got the message and slipped out a few minutes later without a word to anyone.

What made her feel the worst was that this gathering represented her church. Instead of playing the role of the hospitality queen, she had done an "off with his head" number on someone who probably needed to connect with a group like this the most. At the same time, she didn't appreciate that he had "dropped by" or that he had found her through the phone book. She decided right then and there to obtain an unlisted number.

Justin apparently sensed her frustration, especially when she turned the music way down. And being the kind, counselor type, he came over to the couch, sat beside her, and quietly asked questions like: "Is everything okay?" "Did you know Garry was going to show up?" "How are you feeling?"

The minute a twinge of a smile graced Lauren's lips, Justin crossed the room and engaged himself in a conversation with Amy. Lauren watched her, feeling jealous of how unencumbered Amy's life appeared. She seemed free as a bird with a laugh to match. Lauren's laugh used to sound like that. She would give anything to look like that and sound like that again.

It didn't surprise Lauren that Justin left with the others. She didn't expect him to stay and help clean up; although it would have been nice. He invited her to the leadership planning meeting on Monday night, which coincided with her night class, so she said she couldn't make it. What she had hoped was that Justin would follow up with an invitation to do something over the weekend. She even considered inviting him to come back for dinner next weekend. The words never quite made it out of her mouth, and now he was gone.

She comforted herself with the possibility that she would see Justin at work during the week. Maybe he would stop by her teller window. Then it would be natural to invite him to dinner.

Gathering up the paper plates and empty soda cans around her apartment, Lauren began to feel lonely. The trash can under the sink was brimming by the time she stuffed the last of the paper plates into it. The slight smell of tuna fish from the salad lingered in the kitchen, making Lauren wish once again she had a kitten, a soft little creature to keep her company at times like this.

She took her time cleaning up and then began to file

through her CDs, looking for something to cheer her up. Before she could make a selection, the phone rang. It was Mindy.

"Wait till I tell you my outrageous idea for Leon's surprise party on Saturday. This is by far going to be his best birthday ever! You don't have plans for Saturday yet, do you?"

"No." *Unless Justin wants to come for dinner.*

"Good. I want a bunch of people to meet at Jake's — you know, that new tourist trap restaurant where they play old country music. I read in the paper today that this weekend they're offering free meals if you come dressed up like a country-western singer. If we all come dressed up, it won't cost us a thing! Except for Leon. I know he won't come dressed up, but that's okay."

Lauren didn't respond.

"Don't you think it's a great idea?"

"Sure." She faked her enthusiasm.

"What's wrong?"

"Nothing."

"You don't sound like it's nothing."

"It's nothing." Lauren didn't want another sermon from Mindy, and she actually was glad Mindy was preoccupied and hadn't thought to ask Lauren if she had called Jeff. "Tell me more about this wild party."

Mindy dove into all the details she had worked out about their costumes, how they would go early, and how Leon's buddy would drive him there so they could surprise him inside the restaurant.

"Sounds like fun," Lauren said.

"What do you mean 'fun'? It sounds like the hoot of the year. You'll help me pull it off, won't you?"

"Sure, I'll help." Lauren wondered if she would regret her words.

After her conversation with Mindy, Lauren thumbed through a catalog and then decided to check her e-mail. The box on the computer screen showed she had one letter. It was from Brad. Still nothing from KC. Not that it should surprise her. He could still be in Egypt. Or, even more likely, after he had read her last goof-up letter requesting advice from Brad for his lovelorn sister, KC had probably chosen to end their brief but intriguing communication.

Brad's letter read:

WREN, I'M GLAD TO HEAR YOU'RE GOING OUT. GOOD FOR YOU. PLAY THE FIELD. HOLD OUT FOR A HERO. I DISAGREE WITH MINDY ABOUT CALLING JEFF TO GET CLOSURE. YOU CAN HAVE PERSONAL CLOSURE WITHOUT EVER TALKING TO THE DONKEY AGAIN. YOU HAVE TO DECIDE INSIDE YOURSELF THAT YOU'RE OKAY WITH THE RELATIONSHIP BEING OVER. I THINK YOU ALREADY ARE.

DID I TELL YOU I'M TAKING PSYCHOTHERAPEUTIC SYSTEMS THIS SEMESTER? CAN YOU BELIEVE I EVEN KNOW HOW TO SPELL IT? MAYBE I'LL BE BETTER AT COUNSELING YOU AFTER THIS CLASS.

HOW GO YOUR CLASSES?

RAD

It felt good to be able to type back a message saying she hadn't called Jeff and she agreed with Brad's advice. Maybe she had experienced personal closure and didn't realize it. Brad had a lot of insight into relationships for a guy who had remained unattached except for a girlfriend his senior year of high school. That relationship had lasted only for two months — long enough to assure him of a date to the senior prom and short enough to remain unattached when it was time to go away to college.

More than once Lauren had tried to cook up a potential romance for him with one of her friends, but none of them had been right. Brad needed someone a little on the wild side yet settled. Lauren hadn't yet met the right woman for Brad, and obviously neither had he. He wasn't interested in even practicing his dating manners by going out with anyone. Brad told her last June that when the right woman, sent from heaven, walked into his life, he would know it.

As the week progressed, Lauren wished she had her brother's confidence when it came to waiting on God for the right relationship. Justin seemed like such a great guy for her, and she wanted to pursue a relationship. However, as always, it took two to make a relationship.

She was obviously more willing than Justin. He waved at her from the lobby once on Wednesday and passed her in the parking lot in his sweet little "Mabel" on Thursday. When he didn't stop by her teller window on Friday, Lauren decided to call him the minute she got home from work and invite him over for dinner. His answering machine responded to her call. She turned on all her charm at the sound of the beep.

"Hi, Justin. It's Lauren. I guess you've been on the go all week. I wanted to thank you again for dinner at Clementine's and for being such a patient listener. I also appreciated the way you helped me out with the lunch here last Sunday. I was wondering if you would let me thank you properly. I'd like to fix dinner for you sometime this weekend. Tonight is open for me. Or Sunday night. Nothing fancy. We could even rent a video or something if you would like. Give me a call when you have a chance. I hope it works out. Bye."

"Well, that was pointless," she told herself after hanging up. "I'm sure I sounded desperate, saying I was free tonight." She scanned the refrigerator and realized she was in great need of groceries. "What was I planning to fix if he said he could come over tonight?"

The last thing she felt like doing was going out again, especially for groceries. Especially if Justin called in time for them to make popcorn and watch a video.

Slipping into a pair of jeans, Lauren searched for the extra-large sweatshirt she had found at a thrift store. It said, "Don't Mess With Texas." Somehow it seemed like an appropriate thought for her this evening.

Scanning the refrigerator again, Lauren found a bagel, a can of Diet Coke, and a pint of gourmet ice cream in the freezer. Three unique dinner companions. She didn't feel like watching TV. It wouldn't hurt to get a jump on her reading for class. So drowning her loneliness in spoonful after spoonful of double fudge brownie, washed down with Diet Coke, Lauren read the first four chapters in her textbook.

Justin never called back.

She ate the bagel for dessert and went to bed.

Twelve

The next morning Lauren checked her e-mail again, hoping for a letter from KC. The computer spun through its mechanized movements, connecting her with the Internet and displaying her mail box. The number "1" appeared, indicating that a letter was waiting for her. She knew it was from KC:

DEAR WREN (AKA THE MAD E-MAIL BOMBER),

This was the first time he had used the term "dear." Lauren read on, feeling wonderfully warm inside.

LET ME START BY SAYING YOU CERTAINLY MAKE FOR AN INTERESTING PEN PAL. I RETURNED FROM MY TRIP THIS AFTERNOON, AND OF ALL MY MESSAGES, YOURS WAS BY FAR THE ONE WORTH COMING HOME FOR.

SO NOW YOU MUST TELL ME, SINCE I'M INVOLVED IN THIS WHOLE AFFAIR, HOW DID THE DATE GO WITH JUSTIN? AND WHAT ABOUT JEFF? DID YOU CALL HIM AS MINDY SUGGESTED?

AND, IF YOU DON'T MIND MY ASKING, IS BEING A VOLLEY-
BALL MANIAC A GOOD THING IN YOUR BOOK? I HAPPEN TO
HAVE ONLY ONE SPORT. WELL, MAYBE TWO: VOLLEYBALL
AND GOLF. IF YOU HAVE AN AVERSION TO EITHER OF THESE
NOBLE ATHLETIC ENDEAVORS, I'M AFRAID I MIGHT BE
FORCED TO PUT A HALT TO OUR CORRESPONDENCE RIGHT
HERE AND NOW.

THE ACCIDENTAL OPENING OF YOUR HEART TO ME IS CER-
TAINLY NOT A REASON FOR ME TO STOP CONVERSING WITH
YOU. A LACK OF INTEREST IN VOLLEYBALL MIGHT BE.

PEACE, KC

Lauren sat back, smiling and wondering if she were crazy
for liking this nameless, faceless, invisible person.

She typed back to KC:

FEAR NOT, A VOLLEYBALL MANIAC IS A GOOD THING IN
MY BOOK, AND I HAPPEN TO BE ONE. I'M SO GLAD YOU
WROTE BACK. THANKS. SO YOU WANT TO HEAR ALL THE
JUICY DETAILS, HUH? WELL, I RUINED MY DATE WITH
JUSTIN BY BLABBING ABOUT JEFF THE WHOLE TIME, BUT
THEN JUSTIN MET A CHARMING YOUNG LADY AT MY APART-
MENT LAST SUNDAY, AND HE SORT OF VANISHED FROM MY
LIFE.

NO, I DIDN'T CALL JEFF. MY BROTHER THINKS I HAVE TO
SETTLE IT INSIDE MYSELF, NOT IN AN EMOTIONAL CONVER-
SATION WITH JEFF. I AGREE. I'M OVER JEFF. IT WASN'T A
GOOD RELATIONSHIP. I CAN SEE THAT NOW.

BUT I DON'T WANT TO DO TO YOU WHAT I DID TO JUSTIN
LAST FRIDAY NIGHT. SO THAT'S ENOUGH ABOUT JEFF.

I'd love to hear about Egypt. Did you ride a camel or tour a pyramid?

Thanks for writing back. I appreciate you.

Warmly, Wren.

Lauren sent the letter and found she couldn't keep a tender smile from her lips. Checking the refrigerator, ready for breakfast, she decided a trip to the grocery store was unavoidable. So she took off, violating the universal rule of grocery shopping: Never shop on an empty stomach. Hers was worse than empty. Her innards were churning the final remains of double fudge brownie dairy product.

Lauren pulled her car out of the apartment complex and into the flow of traffic. All she could think about was how some people might be content remaining single all their lives, but she dearly wanted to share her life with someone else. Someone she could love with her whole heart.

It bothered her that she felt so happy simply because she had received a letter from KC. No man should have that kind of power over her. She had ridden that roller coaster with Jeff, feeling happy when he was happy, feeling responsible when he was sad. She didn't want to live like that.

I'm going to find my own life. No more of this chasing after attention and being dependent on a man for my happiness. If God has someone for me, he'll have to bring him to my front door!

Lauren smiled at the thought as she pulled into the parking lot of the grocery store and muttered, "So what are my options here? I'm going to marry a pizza delivery boy!"

At the moment, pizza sounded good — anything sounded good. Her cart became fuller and fuller as she ventured down each aisle. And she became hungrier and hungrier. In uncharacteristic style, Lauren tossed all kinds of impulse items into her cart including potato chips, gourmet ice cream, chocolate chips (telling herself she would make cookies that afternoon and take them to work on Monday), and a canister of international-flavored coffee.

She was about to wheel out of the coffee and tea section when a small green box caught her eye. It read, "Irish Breakfast Tea." Lauren stood there for several minutes, holding the box in her hand, trying to remember where she had heard about this tea. Someone told her they liked it. But who?

Into the basket went the green tea box. She would figure out later where the subliminal suggestion had come from. Wherever or whoever it was, the suggestion had had its desired effect.

At the checkout line Lauren tossed in a bag of candy corns from the display. Even though Halloween was more than a month away, evidence of its approach was everywhere. To Lauren, candy corns represented autumn, and she was ready for it to be autumn — ready for a change.

The afternoon wind seemed to cooperate with her wishes as it whipped past her in the parking lot, spinning a french fry box and a plastic coffee cup into a dance of glee.

Lauren paid attention to all the deciduous trees that lined her way home. A few had slight tinges of yellow and orange in their outer leaves. What was it she had read once about autumn trees? Something about their being like gypsies wearing amber jewels in their hair, ready to dance with the wind the moment it came calling. That's how she wanted to live. Like a carefree gypsy, always ready to dance. What a laughable contrast that picture was to her life these past few months, or even this past year as she had planned out her life so carefully with Jeff. Lauren felt as if she was getting back to the old Lauren. The one she liked. The one who had big dreams in high school.

A garage sale sign appeared as she turned the corner toward her apartment complex. Lauren couldn't resist. Leaving her eleven bags of groceries in the backseat of her car, she approached with anticipation the mounds of treasures sprawling across the lawn. Boxes of books and heaps of linens were surrounded by rusty garden tools and crates of canning jars. The old brick manor had probably been there since the turn of the century. The acre or so of surrounding land was circled with new housing developments, one of them being the backside of Lauren's apartment. A young woman sat at a table guarding a metal cash box while an older couple poked around in the clothing stack on the other side of her.

Lauren smiled her greeting and went right to the box of books. She pawed through the vast assortment until she found a small, worn book with roses embossed on the cover. It was entitled *Modern Classics,* which made her chuckle aloud because the copyright date was 1871. The book contained two novels by Nathaniel Hawthorne, *Tales of the White Hills* and *Legends of New England.* Lauren felt her heart beating faster. She had read that Hawthorne had traveled to Italy with his family and actually visited Robert and Elizabeth Browning at Casa Guidi. She clutched the old book, feeling as if she had just met the friend of a dear friend.

The price on the book was a bargain at two dollars. "Excuse me," Lauren said to the young woman at the table. "Do you have any more old books?"

"I'm not sure. We went through a lot of stuff yesterday and this morning. Sold all the furniture. Whatever is out there is what we have left."

"Sounds like quite a sale."

"This was my great-grandparents' home. They both passed away this summer. We're dividing everything up. The property has already been sold."

"What about the house?" Lauren asked, feeling a lump of sorrow in her throat for these people she had never met.

"It's all rundown," the woman said. "I'm sure they'll level it."

"Can't it be moved or saved somehow? Isn't it a historical landmark for this area or anything?"

The woman smiled. "I don't think so. The land is worth far more than the house."

Lauren heartily disagreed, even though she hadn't seen the inside of the house. The imagination wheels began to spin in her head. If she had the money, she would buy the house and fix it up. Maybe turn it into a bed and breakfast. But the balance in her savings account and her monthly income would not qualify her for such a venture.

Some other garage-sale shoppers stepped up with armfuls of clothing. Lauren returned to the linens and drew out of the pile a lovely old wrinkled ivory tablecloth with ivory embroidered flowers in the four corners. She groped through the stack until she had seven matching linen napkins. The eighth napkin eluded her. No matter. When would she have more than seven people over for dinner at the same time?

Returning to the table, Lauren added the linens to her book, feeling jubilant over her finds. She pulled out a ten-dollar bill and handed it to the keeper of the cash.

A little girl on roller blades came clanging up the driveway toward them, carrying an open box in her hands. "I made a sign for them," she said to the woman at the table. "See?"

The box landed on the table in front of Lauren with a thump followed by an echoing chorus of meows.

"Oh, how darling!" Lauren said, reaching inside the box and picking up the kitten that looked the most dazed of the bunch. He fit in the palm of her hand and was the softest little ball of fur she had ever felt. He was mostly gray with two white patches, one on his nose and one on his front right paw. "Are you selling these kittens?" Lauren asked the roller-blade queen.

"Yes, ma'am. They're three dollars each or two for five dollars."

Lauren laughed and said, "I only need one. And this one is worth the price of two to me. Here," she handed the girl the five dollars the woman had given her as change a moment earlier. "Thank you very, very much. I've wanted a kitten for a long time. Does he have a name?"

"No. Only this one does," she said picking up an orange striped tabby. "I call her Pumpkin."

"Well, I hope you find a nice home for Pumpkin."

"I don't. I hope nobody buys her. Maybe then I can keep her." The girl smiled and showed the gap where her two front teeth had been. Lauren wondered if those teeth had come out naturally or if the girl's exuberant roller blading had helped the course of nature.

"Thanks again," Lauren said as she tucked her kitten in the crook of her arm and carried him, with her book and table linens, to the car. "Hi, little one," she said in answer to the kitten's meows. "Are you hungry? I'm starving. Let's get something to eat."

Lauren placed the kitten on the floor in the front of her car and headed back to the grocery store. She pushed the cart down the aisle for the second time that day. This time she picked up cat food and cat box filler and a half dozen other necessities to set up her new house guest. At the deli department she ordered a large roast beef on rye, a bag of Chee-tos, and a large Diet Coke.

Then, balancing her Coke in one hand and scarfing Chee-tos by the handful, Lauren maneuvered her way back to her apartment with the exhausted kitten asleep in her lap, both of them as happy as could be.

Thirteen

❧

Lauren unpacked her groceries with more zest than she had felt in weeks; more than she had felt all summer. Things were changing for her. She was invigorated by the promises of fall, which included an antique book to peruse by the fire and a precious kitten to snuggle with. Perhaps she could tolerate Nashville a little longer and wait patiently for the day when she could move to a small town.

"What should I call you?" she asked her kitten, holding him up to the light. "You're quite a noble looking young man. Sensitive, yet intelligent. Strong, but shy. Tender and very snuggly. All the qualities I look for in a man. Not that I'm looking, though. Not any more. I'm waiting for my pizza-man," she said, rubbing noses with the kitten.

She poured some more milk into the kitten's dish and placed it and the feline on the new mat along the back wall of her kitchen. "So, do you want to hang out with me and wait for the doorbell to ring? It could be a couple of years, you know. You don't have any other plans, do you?

"Good. Neither do I. Except for finishing school. And

reading this book," she said reaching for the Nathaniel Hawthorne book on the counter. "I'll be in the living room. You come snuggle with me when you're finished there, okay?" She stroked the soft fur along his back and watched his tail go straight up in an eager response to her touch.

Lauren turned on the automatic fire in the wall fireplace and curled up on the couch with her dusty volume. It wasn't chilly. Yet Lauren felt such a book should not be explored without a roaring fire.

She dusted the cover with her sleeve. "Nathaniel Hawthorne," she said aloud. "Should I call you Nathaniel? Any friend of Elizabeth's is a friend of mine."

No response came from the kitchen.

"How about Hawthorne? Do you like Hawthorne better?"

The kitten appeared around the corner of the kitchen area, stretching on the carpet and sharpening his claws.

"You like that name, huh? Hawthorne it is. Come here, Hawthorne." She patted her leg, inviting the little one to come join her on the couch. "I probably shouldn't let you up on the furniture, should I? Oh, well. It doesn't matter. I can whip off this cover and wash it any time I want. You belong right here with me."

Hawthorne nuzzled up against her leg. She lifted him to a cozy spot on her lap and turned to the first page. "Shall I read to you, Hawthorne? 'Chapter one, "The Great Stone Face." One afternoon, when the sun was going down, a mother and her little boy sat at the door of their cottage —'"

A knock at her door interrupted their story time.

"Coming." Lauren scooped up Hawthorne and opened the door.

It was Mindy. At least she thought it was Mindy. Her

friend was dressed as a country-western singer with the most ridiculous platinum blond wig Lauren had ever seen.

Lauren slapped her hand over her mouth.

"You forgot," Mindy said, slipping inside the apartment.

Lauren winced and nodded.

"It's only my husband's surprise birthday party," Mindy said with an exaggerated drawl. "Where did you get the cat?"

"This is Hawthorne. I bought him this afternoon at a garage sale. Mindy, I'm sorry. The time got away from me. I'll be ready in five minutes. Seven minutes tops."

"I don't know if I can wait that long," Mindy said, adjusting her voluptuous bosom.

Lauren couldn't hold back the giggles any longer. "What do you have in there? No, never mind. I don't want to know."

"I'll tell ya' a little secret," Mindy said, winking her long false eyelashes and moving closer to Lauren. "It's a little more than what the good Lord endowed me with."

"A little!"

Both women laughed, and Lauren wondered how she ever let Mindy talk her into this crazy scheme.

"I can't wait for you, Lauren. Everyone will be arriving in a few minutes," Mindy said, glancing at her watch over her protruding chest, which was draped in a tight, glittery silver dress.

"Go ahead. I'll meet you there," Lauren said. "I have Leon's present wrapped and everything. I'll be there as quickly as I can."

"Remember to park away from the front of the restaurant so he won't notice your car."

"I will."

"And hurry!"

"I will!" She shut the door as Mindy wiggled her way down the stairs. Then dashing to the bedroom closet, Lauren grabbed her costume and muttered to Hawthorne, "I can't believe I'm going to wear this in public!" She pulled on the simple blue, button-up-the-front dress she had picked up at the same thrift store in which she had found the "Don't Mess With Texas" sweatshirt. Next came ankle socks and clodhopper shoes. With a quick tuck of a few bobby pins, her hair was up. For the final touch, she reached for the hat waiting on the bathroom counter and adjusted it so that the gaudy flowers showed off the most and the long dangling price tag hung down on the right side. She gave herself a big smile and laughed aloud. "No need to bother with makeup," she told herself. With a couple of quick squirts of Vanilla Fields perfume, she was out the door.

At the bottom of the stairs she remembered Leon's gift. She took the stairs in her clunky shoes, two at a time, unlocked the door, and was greeted by Hawthorne's questioning "meow."

"I forgot his present!" she hollered, reaching onto the top shelf in the hall closet and pulling down a large wrapped box. "Okay, I'm really leaving now. You be a good boy, and I'll be back before you have a chance to miss me." She locked the door and hurried to the car.

Driving like a maniac, Lauren arrived in less than ten minutes and spotted an empty parking place right by the front. She whipped into the parking lot, not even noticing a customer who was walking out of the restaurant. She nearly hit him.

He jumped to the side and held up his hands as if surrendering. That's when she noticed it was Justin. The easygoing smile spread across his jaw proved he wasn't upset. Lauren rolled down her window and called out, "Sorry!" She pulled into the empty parking space and hopped out saying, "Are you okay, Justin?"

"I'm fine," he said, coming closer with brows furrowed, trying to figure out who it was who had almost hit him and knew his name. "Lauren?"

"Yes, it's me." She felt self-conscious and silly. So she blurted out, "Pay no attention to the woman behind the funny hat with the dangling price tag." Justin didn't seem to get the joke.

"Are you eating here tonight?" he asked.

"Yes," she said, aware of how ridiculous she must appear to him. "Mindy put together a birthday party for her husband, and we're planning to surprise him."

"I imagine you will."

"Dinner is free, you know, if you dress up like a country-western star," she explained.

"I didn't know that," he said.

"Well, it is. Are you eating here?"

"Yes. As a matter of fact, Amy was supposed to meet me here. I guess I'm a little early."

Lauren felt her heart sink. Here she had planned to make dinner for Justin this weekend, but he had wasted no time in asking Amy out. With intense effort she tried to keep her emotions buoyed up. This was what she had promised herself, wasn't it? No guy would have the power to control her emotions.

"Hey," he said, "I got your message about dinner sometime. Umm, it wouldn't work out for me tomorrow night. I'm not sure —"

"That's okay," Lauren answered quickly. "It was a fleeting thought. I wanted to say thanks, that's all."

"I appreciate it." Justin's dazzling smile led her to believe he had been asked out by more than a few women in his lifetime, and he had found a way to turn on the charm while turning them down. She wasn't interested in being one of many on his long list.

Lauren smiled back and dropped the conversation. She reached back into her car to retrieve Leon's gift off the passenger seat. A car stopped behind Lauren's, and the driver leaned his head and arm out the window and yelled, "Are you coming out?"

She peeked over her shoulder and saw that Leon was in the car.

"Mindy's husband is in that car!" she whispered to Justin. "Tell the driver I'm not leaving. Don't let Leon see me."

"She's not leaving," Justin called out. "There's more parking in the back."

The car moved on. The next car was Amy's.

"Justin!" she called out.

"Hey, Amy!" he answered, walking toward her. "You look really nice tonight."

"I'll go park and meet you at the entrance."

"Okay, darlin'."

Lauren still had her head inside the car. In the darkened quiet she thought, *Is it my imagination, or was Justin calling me "darlin'" only last week?*

She backed out of the car, inwardly gratified she wasn't part of this dating game. "I have to go." She shut her car door with her foot, and with the gift in her arms, she marched past Justin in her orthopedic shoes, clomping her way into the restaurant. He followed right behind and at the door said, "I'm going to wait here for Amy. I'll probably see you in there."

Giving him a "Pearly" smile, she slipped into the lobby and was relieved to see Reba look-alikes and a bevy of Dolly-wannabes. The most humorous one of them all squeaked at her from the side hall that led to the restrooms. "Lauren, what took you so long?" Mindy's wig was crooked, and her ebony hair stuck out from the fake platinum around her forehead. Lauren reached a free hand to straighten it, trying hard not to laugh.

Loud, funky country-western music blared from the belly of the restaurant. "Leon's here!" Lauren said. "He's going to walk through that door any minute. Where's everyone else?"

"In the back. Come on."

They peeked around the corner, checking the front door, and as they did, it opened. In walked, not Leon, but Justin and Amy, hand in hand. Mindy stopped in her tracks and reached over to squeeze Lauren's arm.

"I know," Lauren said calmly. "I saw them in the parking lot. I introduced him to Amy at my apartment last Sunday afternoon. It's okay. Come on, before Leon sees us."

Mindy looked stunned.

Lauren nudged her toward the crowd inside the restaurant. "It's like you always say, 'God is in control,' right?"

"How do you do that?" Mindy said, taking quick, tiny steps next to Lauren and yelling over the music. "You turn your emotions on and off like a faucet. That can't be healthy."

"Oh, so now that I'm trying to trust God, I'm not healthy. Make up your mind, Mindy!"

"Whatever you say, Cleopatra."

"I'm not dressed like Cleopatra," Lauren said.

"Oh, excuse me. I thought you were the queen of de Nile."

"I'm not denying anything!" Lauren said furiously.

Mindy stopped, turned toward her, and said, "You're right. I'm sorry. That wasn't fair."

"Just because my life isn't like yours...," Lauren began. She was stopped when the false eyelash on Mindy's right eye came unglued and fluttered into her cleavage.

"There's a bug in my dress!" Mindy shrieked, beginning to pull out wadded up panty hose and tossing them at Lauren.

Lauren found it difficult to remain upset with a person under such circumstances.

Fourteen

⤜⤏

L eon was more than surprised. Shocked wasn't even quite strong enough a description. Mortified almost hit the mark. Lauren felt sorry for him. He couldn't eat, socialize, or even think straight. He kept staring at his wife, obviously more embarrassed about her appearance than she had ever been about anything in her life.

Mindy moved through the evening undaunted. With her outfit restuffed, she carried the conversation around the table at dinner and was the first to ask the waiter if they had a dessert tray.

Lauren hadn't spotted Justin and Amy the entire evening. The restaurant was large enough that they could have disappeared into some corner booth. Or perhaps they had decided the place was too noisy for a first date and went somewhere quieter. Like Clementine's.

Don't feed yourself that stuff. It'll upset your stomach. And it's not worth it, remember?

The desserts arrived. Leon opened his gifts and was appreciative of them all. He seemed as eager as Lauren to leave. Mindy had other plans. She wanted them all to join the line dancers out on the floor and have a real hoot. It was a hoot, all right. Mindy in her fancy dress and wild wig, Lauren in her clodhoppers and floppy hat, and the rest of the group, who all had chickened out and had come dressed as they normally did.

Lauren ended up in line with a Garth look-alike and two big-haired Rebas. What made the whole experience so fun and crazy was that the music at Jake's was country-western hits from the '50s and '60s. Leon began to enjoy himself and actually ended up begging Mindy to stay for "just one more" about eight times.

Exhausted, but still smiling, Lauren arrived home after midnight. Hawthorne was curled up in his new bed by the fireplace and didn't budge when she came in. However, he had obviously been busy while she was gone. Shredded papers were scattered on the floor, twisted blinds hung from the windows, his milk dish had been dumped, and the rose-colored cover on her easy chair had nearly been pulled off.

"So you had a wild party while I was out, did you?" She stroked his fur, and he began to purr. "I guess that's all part of the deal. You keep me company, and I endure your rambunctious years. I can live with that. Just try to not break anything, okay?"

Even though she was tired, the computer beckoned her to turn it on and check her e-mail. She felt like a compulsive gambler, unable to walk past a slot machine without dropping in a nickel. She turned on the computer and went into the kitchen to heat up some water and make herself something hot to drink. The Irish Breakfast tea caught her eye, and she decided to try it. Something in her memory said to drink it with milk and sugar, so she placed those items on the kitchen counter. The microwave beeped, signaling that her water was ready. She poured the steaming water over her tea bag, steeped it a few minutes, and then added the milk and sugar. It smelled wonderful.

"Okay," Lauren said to her sleeping kitten as she headed to the computer with a cup of tea and a bowl of candy corns, "a little midnight snack and hopefully a letter."

There it was. Just as she had hoped. She nibbled off the white tip of a candy corn and began to read:

DEAR WREN:

THANKS FOR YOU LETTER. I APPRECIATE YOU, TOO. AS FOR THE CAMEL RIDE, YES AND NO. I DIDN'T GO FOR AN ACTUAL RIDE, BUT I DID HAVE MY PHOTO TAKEN ON ONE WITH THE PYRAMIDS IN THE BACKGROUND. IT'S QUITE THE TOURIST THING TO DO. THE REST OF MY TIME IN EGYPT WAS ALL MEETINGS AND INTERVIEWS AND HOTEL FOOD. NOTHING NEARLY AS INTERESTING AS YOUR TURN OF EVENTS WITH JUSTIN. ARE THINGS PROGRESSING WITH HIM AND THE YOUNG LADY?

YOUR BROTHER COULD BE RIGHT ABOUT RESOLVING ISSUES WITHIN YOURSELF. AT LEAST THAT'S A GOOD PLACE TO START — IN YOUR HEART, BETWEEN YOU AND GOD. I'LL PRAY THAT YOU EXPERIENCE A NEW LEVEL OF PEACE IN CHRIST. I'M A FIRM BELIEVER IN THE PEACE OF CHRIST AND OUR POSITION AS SAINTS TO PRAY FOR THAT PEACE TO COME TO OTHERS.

MAY THE PEACE OF CHRIST SURROUND YOU, KC

Lauren found her heart pounding and a smile resting on

her lips like a pink satin ribbon. KC's words had a powerful effect on her. She sipped her tea, and then it came to her. KC was the one who had recommended Irish Breakfast with milk and sugar.

Trying another sip, she decided this was the tea for her. It even tasted better than coffee. She had to tell him. With another sip of her soothing tea, Lauren tapped out her reply:

DEAR KC:

I'VE JUST RETURNED FROM A SURPRISE BIRTHDAY PARTY FOR MY FRIEND'S HUSBAND. GUESS WHO WAS AT THE RESTAURANT? JUSTIN AND AMY. HOLDING HANDS, EVEN. THEY MAKE A DARLING COUPLE. I SAY, "BRAVO AND MAY THE PEACE OF CHRIST BE UPON THEM."

THIS WAS A FULL DAY. I FOUND A GARAGE SALE AND BOUGHT A NATHANIEL HAWTHORNE BOOK (DID YOU KNOW HE VISITED ROBERT AND ELIZABETH AT CASA GUIDI?), SOME ELEGANT TABLE LINENS, AND THE CUTEST KITTEN THIS SIDE OF THE MISSISSIPPI.

AND JUST TO LET YOU KNOW HOW MUCH YOU'RE INFLUENCING MY LIFE, AT THIS VERY MOMENT I AM DRINKING A CUP OF IRISH BREAKFAST TEA WITH MILK AND SUGAR. MY FIRST EVER, AND WHAT A DELIGHTFUL EXPERIENCE IT IS. THANKS FOR THE TIP. NOW YOU MUST TELL ME: DID THEY HAVE ANY IRISH BREAKFAST IN EGYPT?

SMILES, WREN

With a tap of a few keys her letter was sent. Lauren prepared a short note for Brad, telling him about Hawthorne, and sent it off to him within five minutes. She was about to close down her computer when she noticed she had a letter waiting for her. Checking her box, she found a second letter from KC. Amazing! It was after one o'clock in the morning her time, and wherever KC was, he was at this very moment sitting at his computer, and the minute he had received her letter, he had turned around and written her back:

DEAR WREN,

ARE YOU A NIGHT-OWL, TOO? I SHOULD BE FINISHING AN ARTICLE I'M WORKING ON FOR AN EARLY MORNING DEADLINE, BUT SPENDING SOME TIME CHATTING WITH YOU IS MUCH MORE APPEALING. TO ANSWER YOUR QUESTION, I HAD TO TAKE MY OWN TEA TO EGYPT, BUT I USUALLY DO THAT ANYWAY.

I HAVEN'T BEEN TO A GOOD GARAGE SALE IN AGES. A CAT, HUH?

YOUR BOOK SOUNDS INTRIGUING. I HAVE TO ADMIT I'M NOT SURE I'VE EVER READ ANY HAWTHORNE. DICKENS IS MY MAN. I HAVE A FIRST EDITION OF *A TALE OF TWO CITIES*, WHICH I UNDERSTAND MIGHT BE WORTH SOMETHING. I'LL NEVER SELL IT, THOUGH.

DO YOU SUPPOSE DICKENS AND HAWTHORNE MIGHT HAVE E-MAILED EACH OTHER, IF THE TECHNOLOGY HAD EXISTED THEN? I DO KNOW THAT RALPH WALDO EMERSON AND THOMAS CARLYLE KEPT A CORRESPONDENCE GOING FOR YEARS. I GUESS KINDRED SPIRITS FIND EACH OTHER AND ARE DRAWN BACK TIME AND AGAIN THROUGH LETTERS. I CERTAINLY LOOK FORWARD TO YOURS. KEEP 'EM COMING.

PEACE, KC

If she had any hesitation about opening up to this man before, that concern had flown. The opportunity for a non-threatening, stimulating relationship with this unknown man felt safe and wonderfully romantic.

In the months that followed, without anyone else knowing about this correspondence, Lauren launched into consistent communication with KC, discussing volleyball, literature, music, movies, friends, family, and God. She noted the subject of cats didn't come up again, and she wondered if KC approved of cats. She hoped he did.

Fifteen

❧

A chill winter wind chased Lauren across the campus of Belmont University. In her right hand she clutched her admissions papers. It wasn't likely that she would be admitted at this late date for the next semester, but she was ready to plead her case. She had just learned a few days ago that only Belmont offered the upper division course she needed before she could apply for her teaching credential in Tennessee. She had come this far in her schooling, and she didn't want to stop now.

Striding through the center of the campus, Lauren couldn't help but notice the big white gazebo with elaborate ironwork and scrolled pillars. A couple bundled in long coats stood close together in the center, their laughter echoing off the dome ceiling. She smiled at the young couple and kept walking. They were in the spring of their relationship, and they were standing in the gazebo the hairstylist-hacker had told Lauren about last summer. Thoughts of Jeff and planning their wedding in a gazebo were far, far away, buried beneath the cold winter turf. That all had happened during another time when she was another person.

Lauren found the admissions office, turned in her paperwork, set an appointment to talk with an admissions counselor the next week, and walked briskly back to her car. A light snow began to fall as she pulled out of the parking lot. The Friday evening traffic was a mess, and Lauren wondered if she should try to run some more errands before going home. Christmas was in two weeks, and she hadn't finished her shopping yet.

As the windshield wipers furiously fought to keep her window clear, Lauren signaled for a right turn into a strip mall shopping center. She turned in and noticed a scruffy looking man poking around in the dumpster.

Lauren parked and dashed into the dry cleaners to pick up her clothes. Writing out the check for the four cleaned items, she thought of the man. He was probably homeless. She did a rough calculation of how many meals could be purchased for the outrageous amount she was paying for her dry cleaning. It bothered her.

Unlocking her car and hanging the clothes on the hook in the back, Lauren noticed the man was now standing under the sheltering eaves of the video store next to the dry cleaners. He looked cold.

Lauren got in her car and, with a sense of purpose, drove to the Long John Silver's fast food restaurant across the street. She waited in a long line before ordering enough food for two, or maybe even three, people. With the bag of hot food beside her in the front seat, she drove through the busy intersection and parked in the snow sprinkled parking lot.

The man was no longer by the video store. She drove slowly, checking out the dumpster area and the dark alley between the hardware store and the insurance office. Something moved in the alley.

Lauren slung her purse over her shoulder, reached into her glove compartment, took out her leather gloves, a gift from Jeff last Valentine's Day, and tucked them into the sack of hot food. Then, carefully balancing the large coffee in one hand and the bag of food between her teeth, Lauren used her free hand to lock her door and then to pocket her keys.

No one was around as she ventured into the dark alley. Silent snowflakes caught a ride on her hair and shoulders, offering quiet comfort.

"Hello?" she called out in small but cheery voice.

The man rose from his huddled position against the wall.

"I, um...I brought you some dinner." She held out the bag and the coffee cup.

The man stared at her without moving a muscle.

"There's, um, creamer and sugar in the bag if you don't like your coffee black." Lauren held it out closer to him.

The man looked both directions. In one swift movement, he pulled something from his belt and in a gravelly voice ordered, "Gimme your purse."

"Excuse me?" Lauren couldn't believe her ears.

She did believe her eyes when the blade of the vagrant's six-inch knife caught the light from the yellow security lamp.

"Give it to me, now!" he shouted.

Too startled to do anything else, Lauren put down the food and coffee and quickly slipped her purse strap over her shoulder. The man snatched it from her and took off running.

Lauren stood there, dumbfounded. She checked her pocket. Her car keys were still there. At least he couldn't steal her car, too.

"I've been robbed," she muttered, looking down at the food. "I brought him dinner, and he stole my purse." Dazed, she made her way back to her car, opened the door, climbed in, locked the doors, and sat there. She held the bag of food in her lap but knew she could never eat any of it. "I can't believe this."

Should she call the police? Go tell someone? How would she explain that she had entered the dark alley at night, knowing a questionable character was lurking there, and now she was actually surprised at the outcome. Any police officer would call her foolish.

Forgoing the rest of her errands, Lauren started the car and inched her way home on the slick streets. She shook her head and muttered to herself all the way.

Hawthorne's eager "meow" as she unlocked her apartment door brought her sweet comfort. She lifted the medium-sized cat and took him with her to the couch where she sat for a long time, stroking his fur and allowing his contented purring to calm her nerves.

It was after eight before she got up and fixed herself a cup of tea. She opened a can of cat food for Hawthorne and said, "At least you won't turn on me when I offer you some dinner."

Reaching for the phone, she finally dialed the local police. The officer who took her report was understanding when she described the circumstances. He advised her to cancel all her credit cards right away, close her bank account, and call the DMV on Monday. Then he added in a fatherly tone, "I know you thought you were doing the right thing, miss. I understand your goodwill toward men, being that it's Christmastime and all. It's a sad world we live in when a person can't be neighborly. I only hope this unpleasant experience will serve you well in the future and protect you from an even greater harm."

"Thank you," Lauren said. "Good night."

She hung up and decided to pick up her mail before it became much darker. Her mom had said last week that she was sending Lauren plane tickets so she could come home for Christmas. Tucking Hawthorne under her arm for protection, Lauren scanned the apartment parking lot as she carefully descended the snow covered stairs. The common mailbox was only ten steps from the bottom of her stairs. She had never been afraid of going there at night before. But then, she had never been robbed before, either. Lauren stuck her key in the slot, quickly unlocked her box, extracted a few letters, and hopped through the snow back to her apartment.

She turned on the gas fireplace and curled up with Hawthorne to read her mail. She had received four Christmas cards. One was from her old college roommate, Teri. Lauren opened it, read the few lines scrawled at the bottom, and bit her lower lip. Teri didn't know about Jeff. She said she was looking forward to coming to Nashville for their February wedding. Teri was older than Lauren, had graduated two years before her, and was doing exactly what Lauren wished she were — teaching in a small town.

Forcing herself to the phone, Lauren looked up Teri's number and glanced at the clock. It was around dinnertime in Oregon where Teri lived. Lauren began to dial. It was Friday night. Teri hadn't mentioned dating anyone. All her card said was that she had spent the summer with her sister on Maui. Chances were she would be home.

A strangely deep and froggy voice answered.

"Is Teri there?"

"This is Teri," the raspy voice said.

"Is Teri Moreno there?"

"It's me," the voice barked. "I have laryngitis."

"Oh, Teri, you sound awful. It's Lauren. I hope I'm not bothering you." Lauren hoped she hadn't gotten Teri out of bed. Had the raspy voice startled Lauren more than it should have because of her bad experience that night in the alley?

"How are you?" Teri said. Her words sounded painful. Lauren decided this would be a quick call.

"Well, actually," Lauren chose to skip the mugging story and make this a casual conversation, "I'm doing quite well."

"Good!"

"I received your Christmas card," Lauren continued. "And I realized I hadn't talked to you in a long time, so you don't know what's happening in my life. I was going to write you, but then I thought it would be easier if I called."

"Let me guess," Teri whispered. "You've moved up the wedding date."

Lauren paused before saying, "Actually, Jeff and I broke up. I should have told you sooner, but I didn't realize until I received your Christmas card that you didn't know."

"Oh, Lauren, I'm sorry!" Teri finally said.

Lauren didn't know if it was the emotional drain from the theft or the memories of Jeff that had slightly thawed when she saw the gazebo today, but she felt all her defenses melt when she heard Teri's response. "I am, too," Lauren said in a whisper laced with pain.

Sixteen

❧

auren recovered quickly from her brief display of grief over Jeff. She wrote to KC about her experience with the homeless man but flew to her parents' home in Victoria, British Columbia, for Christmas before she heard back from KC. She had a wonderful time with her parents and Brad and more than once nearly told them about her correspondence with KC. Each time, something stopped her. What she and KC had was so close, so private, that she wasn't ready to tell anyone in the event that person might spoil it for her.

When she arrived back in Nashville, four electronic letters were waiting for her. All from KC, all warm and tender. He said he had thought about her on Christmas Eve:

...MY BROTHER WAS MAKING JOKES ABOUT HOW I CARRY MY LAPTOP EVERYWHERE I GO. HE SAID IT WAS MY "SONAR" DEVICE AND THAT I SEND OUT SIGNALS TO RECEIVE A RESPONSE FROM THE MOTHER SHIP. I THOUGHT ABOUT HOW I SEND OUT A MESSAGE, AND YOU ELECTRONICALLY ECHO BACK. IT'S A WONDERFUL THING! YOU CAN'T IMAGINE HOW SOLITARY MY LIFE HAS BECOME. THE LONELY

JOURNALIST, SENDING OUT MESSAGES TO OTHER PARTS OF THE WORLD, BUT ONLY ONE — YOURS — RETURNS TO ME, ECHOING MY HEART.

Through the rest of the winter and into the spring, KC and Wren continued to echo each others' hearts. He seemed to be traveling more, and she was holed up in her apartment nearly every weekend with her homework, reading with Hawthorne on her lap and sipping Irish Breakfast.

In March, KC sent a letter telling Lauren about a devotional book his brother had given him called *My Utmost for His Highest* by Oswald Chambers. KC referred to the entry for March 22, which was based on a portion of Luke 24:32, "Did not our heart burn within us...?" KC asked Lauren if she could buy the devotional book and tell him what she thought of that entry.

Lauren stopped at the Christian bookstore the next day on her way home from work. Not only did she buy a copy of the book, but she also bought three CDs, a gift book, a Bible study guide, and two novels. With all her studying, she had read little for pleasure. The time had come for an evening in the tub with an inspirational romance novel and a new CD.

She read the devotional first that evening. Both the entry for March 22 and the one for that day, March 23. The words hit her right where she had struggled in the past — with controlling her emotions. She had plenty of thoughts to communicate to KC on the topic and wrote him before indulging herself with a bubble bath and one of her new novels.

During the following two weeks they wrote each other every day, always commenting on the devotion for that day from their shared book. It struck Lauren as romantic to know that when she was reading the Scripture for that day, somewhere in the world KC was on the same page, reading the same words. Often their thoughts coincided on the daily reading. Many times one or the other would bring up a new thought, and so they sharpened each other spiritually.

The intense spiritual discussion was broken in April when KC went on a business trip and didn't e-mail Lauren for nine days. She felt lost without his correspondence and afraid of the level of intensity to which their relationship had risen. She thought it was time to evaluate where they were in their relationship. However, KC didn't see the need to dissect "them." So she backed off.

Then, as a wave that has receded returns, cresting higher than the last time, their intimacy began to build during the end of June.

On July 6, Lauren drew up all her courage and wrote:

DEAR KC,

HAPPY ANNIVERSARY, MY DEAR FRIEND! DID YOU KNOW IT WAS A YEAR AGO TODAY THAT MY BROTHER "INTRODUCED" US? CAN YOU BELIEVE IT HAS BEEN A WHOLE YEAR? SO, WHEN DO WE MEET FACE TO FACE? I WANT TO SEE YOUR EYES AND HEAR YOUR VOICE. I WANT TO SLIP MY HAND INTO YOURS.

Lauren reread her words, and something in the pit of her stomach began to churn. Did she truly want to meet him and end the masquerade? So many times she had thought about what it would be like to finally meet. So many times she had written something to that effect in one of her letters, only to erase it before sending the letter. She always ended up deciding it would be better to wait. Wait for what? She wasn't sure. Perhaps wait for KC to initiate the meeting. Or for it to somehow just happen.

Whenever she thought about it logically, Lauren found she had no complaints about how nice and slow everything had gone. It gave her time to do some important things. First, she had gotten over Jeff. She still felt twinges of hurt every now and then. But she wasn't afraid of them. They were only evidence of healing, KC had once written to her. He said scars still tend to pinch even after they're healed, if they're pulled the wrong way.

Second, she had finished school. She had filed the final paperwork two weeks ago and was now qualified to teach. However, she wasn't ready to leave her job at the bank just yet. Not since she had received a raise two months ago. Also, Lauren wasn't sure she wanted to teach in a public school in the city. She still held to her dream of living in a small town. Her preference would be to teach at a small school. Someday.

And the third reason Lauren was glad her relationship with KC was correspondence only was because she had gained weight. Ten pounds since Christmas and a total of nearly fifteen since Jeff broke up with her last summer. It had been a cold winter, and she had comforted herself by the fire with cookies, sweets, and lots of Irish Breakfast with milk and sugar. Lauren had also spent most of her evenings and weekends studying and had exercised little. She had finally given in and accepted her new shape at the beginning of the summer, forcing herself to buy some clothes that fit, even though she wasn't happy with her thickened waist.

The worst part was that no one seemed to agree with her that she had gained too much weight. They all, including Brad, said she had been too skinny before. That idea was a struggle for Lauren. She had lost ten pounds when she started to date Jeff and had consciously tried to keep herself thin because she knew that was how he liked her. Now she was more rounded. More average looking.

It was funny, but she had dreamed more than once that she and KC met and she looked the way she used to, with her long blond hair and cinched waist. She never could see his face in her dreams, and she would awaken each time, groping in the darkness, desperate to see his expression. Was he disappointed that she was an average woman with average short blond hair and average features? What always pulled Lauren out of the emotional bog those thoughts sent her into was that she liked herself so much more than she had liked the old Lauren who was always apologizing and feeling like a failure.

Returning her attention to her letter, she went back and deleted the part about meeting and concluded the letter with:

IT'S BEEN A WONDERFUL YEAR. YOU HAVE BEEN A GIFT FROM GOD TO ME.

ALWAYS, WREN

The letter was sent, and Lauren asked Hawthorne if he wanted to go with her to pick up the mail. Hawthorne, who had grown into a fat, sassy plutocrat, stretched on his front haunches and yawned as if to show his disinterest. He had turned into a lazy old house cat and had little desire to venture outside his air-conditioned domain.

Lauren slipped on a pair of sandals and went to the mailbox alone. The summer afternoon sky canopied her in vivid blue. It was hot. Sticky hot. Lauren unlocked her mail box. Inside were two fancy white envelopes sitting side by side.

145

She guessed they were wedding invitations.

One, she surmised, would be from Justin and Amy. They had announced their engagement several months ago in front of the career group at church. Justin said in front of everyone he would always be grateful to Lauren for bringing him and Amy together. Lauren was fine with that. Over the months she had enjoyed the company of both Justin and Amy as friends. They had come over for dinner a few times, and Lauren had even doubled with them once when Justin's cousin was in town. That turned out to be a mistake. But her friendship with Justin and Amy as a couple was comfortable and important to her.

On her way up the stairs, she opened the first invitation. It was from Justin and Amy, all right. It looked like something Amy would choose: embossed flowers with a pink tinge and a matching pink liner inside the envelope.

The next invitation had a return address of Escondido, California. Lauren slid her fingernail under the seal, wondering who she knew in Escondido, of all places. She couldn't think of anyone.

Entering the apartment and breathing in the cooled air, she pulled out the simple yet elegant parchment invitation and scanned the script for a familiar name. There it was: Teresa Angelina Raquel Moreno.

"Teri?" Lauren said aloud, dropping into the nearest kitchen chair. Hawthorne came over and rubbed against her leg. "I can't believe it, Hawthorne. Even my old college roommate is getting married! I talked to her at Christmas, and she didn't say anything about dating someone."

Lauren read the invitation again. "Gordon Thomas Allistar. How's that for a name? Where did she find this guy?

What's happening to me, Hawthorne? All my friends are getting married!"

Jamming the invitations back into their envelopes, Lauren returned to the computer, muttering, "That does it, Hawthorne. I'm going to tell KC it's time we meet. Put up or shut up, that's what I'll say."

She tapped out a letter which sounded more like an ultimatum than a romantic invitation to a rendezvous, and immediately erased it. Her anniversary letter had been sent. That was enough for one day. She needed to focus her mind on something else.

That was the problem. For so long she had had reading assignments, papers, and exams hanging over her head every evening and weekend. Now she was done, and her free time was filled with too many unscheduled hours.

Turning off the computer, Lauren opened the bottom drawer of her desk and pulled out a white, three-ring binder full of papers. They were all KC's letters. She had printed them out about three months ago and put them, nice and tidy, in a binder. If Mindy or Brad or her parents ever knew about this, they would think she was nuts. That's why her secret had remained her secret and probably why it was such a sweet one.

CHAPTER

*S*eventeen

❧

With her treasured collection of love letters in her lap, Lauren turned to the front page. There she had made long lists of what the initials "KC" could possibly stand for. The wildest option was "Kevin Costner" and the quirkiest possibility was "Kamlish Castleman," a boy who had sat behind her in third grade and had come to the States from Fiji. She remembered his long fingers and the strange foods he used to bring in his lunch.

More likely KC was someone she had never met who had a nice normal name and came from a nice normal family. That's what she wanted to believe. Desperately, she wanted to believe that.

Lauren turned the pages past the first few letters from KC and stopped at one from late November:

DEAR WREN,

I MUST TELL YOU HOW MUCH YOUR CORRESPONDENCE HAS MEANT TO ME. I'VE KEPT MYSELF FROM ANY SERIOUS RELATIONSHIPS FOR QUITE SOME TIME. MY JOB TAKES UP ALL MY

ENERGY. HOWEVER, I WANT YOU TO KNOW THAT YOUR LETTERS ARE WHAT I LOOK FOR FIRST WHEN I COME HOME. I ENJOY SPENDING TIME WITH YOU, AS IT WERE.

I APPRECIATED YOUR ADVICE ABOUT VISITING THE HUNTINGTON LIBRARY WHEN I WAS IN SOUTHERN CALIFORNIA LAST WEEK. YOU WERE RIGHT. THE *GUTENBERG BIBLE* HELD ME CAPTIVE FOR QUITE SOME TIME. MY, HOW FAR WE'VE COME IN PRINTING TECHNOLOGY. YET HAVE WE LOST SOME OF THE BEAUTY OF THE "PREPARED" PAGE? RED DYE FROM BERRIES TO STAIN THE PICTURES ON EACH PAGE, DID YOU SEE THAT? AND IT HAS LASTED FOR CENTURIES. BEING IN THE PRINT MEDIA BUSINESS, I CAN'T HELP BUT WONDER HOW LONG SOME OF MY WORDS WILL LAST.

PEACE, KC

Lauren smiled, thinking that if KC only knew how his words were bound in her notebook and carried around in her mind every day, he would know that his words, at least his words to her, had timeless value.

Skimming a few more letters, Lauren wondered if this could be considered an obsession. Would her friends and family urge her to get counseling if they knew how attached she had become to this nameless, faceless person? Was this the ultimate for Generation X: deeply emotional relationships carried on through electronic impulses that course through the computer rather than the body?

Perhaps the most appealing part was the lack of commitment necessary for such a relationship. This was nonthreatening. None of the irritable mannerisms of the other person came into play. The physical dimension wasn't even an issue.

Everything that happened between Lauren and KC went from heart to heart with no fleshly, physical complications. This was an appealing relationship for a Christian woman who desired to remain pure.

Yet it was so much more intense than anything she had ever experienced with any other man. KC had access to her soul, the place deep within her where she thought and mused and loved God and questioned life. And she had access to his innermost being as well.

How did that happen? It wasn't simply because they corresponded. Was it the result of the course their communication had taken? The way they conversed about things that mattered the most to them, and on every score discovered commonality? These questions rolled through her mind with no one to discuss them with.

She turned to another letter in her notebook dated February 14, Valentine's Day. Lauren remembered how she had carefully chosen some lines from Elizabeth Barrett Browning's *Sonnets of the Portuguese* as her Valentine's Day "gift" for KC. She had e-mailed his letter the night before so he would be sure to read it on the fourteenth:

DEAR KC,

I WANTED TO SEND YOU SOMETHING FOR VALENTINE'S DAY AND FOUND THESE WORDS FROM OUR FRIEND EBB ECHOED MY THOUGHTS NICELY:

THE FACE OF ALL THE WORLD IS CHANGED I THINK,
SINCE FIRST I HEARD THE FOOTSTEPS OF THY SOUL
MOVE STILL, OH STILL, BESIDE ME...
...MET IN THEE, AND FROM OUT THEE OVERCAME
MY SOUL WITH SATISFACTION OF ALL WANTS:

BECAUSE GOD'S GIFTS PUT MAN'S BEST DREAMS TO SHAME.

YOUR FRIENDSHIP HAS BEEN A GIFT TO ME FROM GOD, KC.
YOU TIPTOED IN AT A TIME WHEN ALL MY DREAMS WERE
BEING PUT TO SHAME. I LIKE THE WAY MY LIFE HAS
CHANGED, AND YOU'VE HAD A PART IN THAT. THANK YOU
AND HAPPY VALENTINE'S DAY!

ALWAYS, WREN

His Valentine's Day response had been as specifically affectionate for her as hers had been for him. She ran her hand over the next page where the printed characters looked as ordinary as any other arrangement of the alphabet, only this was far different. Hope sprang from these words. They were KC's words, and they had melded themselves into her heart:

DEAR WREN,

YOUR VALENTINE THOUGHTS FROM EBB WARMED ME THIS
MORNING. I HAVE A HUGE ASSIGNMENT TO GET AT. THE
DEADLINE IS TOMORROW, AND I KNOW I'LL SPEND HALF
THE DAY ON THE PHONE. SO BEFORE THE SWEET GLOW OF
YOUR LETTER FADES, LET ME SEND TO YOU MY VALENTINE
WISH. I RESPECTFULLY ECHO THE POETIC SENTIMENT OF
OUR FRIEND, ROBERT BROWNING:

THEN WE BEGAN TO RIDE. MY SOUL
SMOOTHED ITSELF OUT, A LONG-CRAMPED SCROLL
FRESHENING AND FLUTTERING IN THE WIND. . .
WHAT IF WE STILL RIDE ON, WE TWO,
WITH LIFE FOREVER OLD YET NEW,
CHANGED NOT IN KIND BUT IN DEGREE,
THE INSTANT MADE ETERNITY

I, TOO, HAVE BENEFITED GREATLY FROM OUR "RIDE"
TOGETHER ON THE NET. YOU'VE PROVIDED A PLACE FOR
THE REAL ME TO FRESHEN AND FLUTTER IN THE WIND.
THANK YOU, WREN. I FIND I MUST BE HONEST AND SIGN
THIS,

YOURS, KC

From that day on, she had begun to believe that he was
hers. Next she turned to the letter he wrote in April after his
trip to England when she had waited nine days for his
response:

DEAR WREN,

I CAN'T BELIEVE HOW MUCH I'VE MISSED YOU. ALTHOUGH I
SHOULDN'T BE SURPRISED. YOU'VE BECOME SO MUCH A
PART OF MY EVERYDAY LIFE. I SUPPOSE WE SHOULD BE
ALARMED AT OUR CONNECTEDNESS. WHAT WOULD I EVER
DO IF PRINCE CHARMING WALKED INTO YOUR LIFE AND
TOOK YOU AWAY FROM ME?

I MUST TELL YOU ABOUT MY TRIP. HAVE YOU EVER BEEN TO
LONDON IN THE SPRING? TO QUOTE OUR MAN, ROBERT:

OH TO BE IN ENGLAND, NOW THAT APRIL'S THERE,
AND WHOEVER WAKES IN ENGLAND SEES, SOME MORNING,
UNAWARE...

I CAN'T REMEMBER THE REST. BUT I CERTAINLY SAW THE
REST LAST WEEK. I HIT A PARTICULARLY WARM SPELL MY
LAST TWO DAYS THERE, AND THE GARDENS WERE BURSTING
WITH LIFE AND COLOR. WONDERFUL!

I STOPPED FOR TEA IN THE CHELSEA DISTRICT AND THEN
WALKED FOR BLOCKS IN THE FRESH SUNSHINE. I FOUND A

CHAPEL — ST. LUKE'S, I BELIEVE. THE GARDEN THERE WAS LAUGHING IN RED TULIPS. YOU SHOULD HAVE SEEN THEM, ROLLING WITH HILARITY IN THAT DEEP GREEN GRASS.

I STROLLED THROUGH THE MIDDLE OF THEIR PARTY, NODDING TO EACH ONE AS I PASSED, AND THEN I ENTERED THE CHAPEL WHERE ALL WAS QUIET. IN THAT HOLY PLACE I FELT THE PRESENCE OF CHRIST, WHICH WAS A GREAT COMFORT TO ME THAT DAY.

NO ANGELS DANCED BEFORE ME. NO BELLS CHIMED. IT WAS JUST HIS PRESENCE, HIS UNMISTAKABLE PRESENCE IN THAT CHAPEL AND IN MY LIFE. I KNEW I COULD TRUST HIM FOR ALL, INCLUDING THE FUTURE OF "US." HAVE YOU FELT THAT SAME PEACE? A QUIET CONFIDENCE THAT FOR RIGHT NOW, THIS IS ALL WE NEED. A SHARING OF OUR SOULS. "IN QUIETNESS AND CONFIDENCE SHALL BE YOUR PEACE."

I'D LIKE TO HEAR YOUR THOUGHTS.

YOURS, KC

Lauren had written back that she felt comfortable with where things were right then, even though she couldn't say she had ever felt a special peace or presence of the Lord regarding this. However, she wondered if they needed to spend some time trying to evaluate where they were going and what they should expect from the other.

KC's one-line response the next day was:

WREN: LET IT BE. LOVE, KC

She decided she was smitten. How could she help but fall in love with a man who could quote Robert Browning, Isaiah, and the Beatles with such eloquence?

Eighteen

auren didn't hear back from KC after her July "anniversary" letter for two full days. She came home from work on Tuesday evening, ready for a glass of iced tea and a nap on the couch. Outside, the summer weather was cranking up. Inside, Hawthorne greeted her with a plea for food and a look that said he didn't know what day of the week it was or what month of the year. He lived in a climate-controlled environment in which all his meals were delivered at the drop of a "meow." What did he have to worry about?

"You know, you're costing me money, big boy. My electric bill is going to be gigantic this month. What if I leave the air conditioning off tomorrow and open the window?" She knew she couldn't do that to the pampered baby.

"You need a life, Hawthorne. I'm going to start taking you for walks. Look how flabby you're getting."

"Meow," said Hawthorne, which meant, *Your threats are always empty ones, my dear.*

"Then I'll get you a kitten to look after. How would you like that?"

Disinterested in any of her suggestions, Hawthorne stuck

up his tail at her as he began to consume his dinner.

Lauren poured herself a tall glass of iced Irish Breakfast tea, which was waiting for her in a pitcher in the refrigerator. She settled in by the computer, delighted to find the number "2" in her e-mail letter box.

She opened Brad's letter first. He didn't have much to say. His summer school courses were boring, and he was thinking about going on an outreach to Mexico in August with a bunch of guys from his Sunday school class. He asked her to send him the dates she would be in California for her friend's wedding.

Lauren replied:

I BOUGHT MY PLANE TICKETS YESTERDAY. TERI'S WEDDING IS IN ESCONDIDO ON SATURDAY, AUGUST 3.

She felt a twinge in her heart, remembering that her wedding date had been set for February 3. Six months ago. So much had happened since. She had changed dramatically. At this moment, Lauren couldn't imagine herself married to Jeff. How different a person she would have become. Not necessarily bad, just vastly different. She liked who she was now and where her life was going.

I'LL FLY INTO BURBANK ON FRIDAY NIGHT AND PICK UP A RENTAL CAR. I SHOULD REACH YOUR PLACE BEFORE NINE. CAN I STAY WITH YOU THAT NIGHT? I NEED TO LEAVE AROUND NINE IN THE MORNING; THEN I'LL BE BACK AGAIN LATE SATURDAY NIGHT. IF YOU'RE REAL NICE, I'LL LET YOU TAKE ME TO BRUNCH AFTER CHURCH ON SUNDAY. MY PLANE LEAVES AT THREE THAT AFTERNOON. PLEASE TELL ME THIS FITS INTO YOUR DEMANDING SCHEDULE.

LAUREN

Sending it off with the push of a button, Lauren eagerly opened KC's letter.

DEAR WREN,

A WHOLE YEAR, HUH? MY, TIME FLIES WHETHER YOU'RE HAVING FUN OR NOT. LATELY I HAVEN'T BEEN HAVING FUN. I'VE BEEN TRAVELING AGAIN, AND I RETURNED TO AN UNBELIEVABLE MOUND OF WORK. I'LL BE UP ALL NIGHT TRYING TO MEET THIS DEADLINE. I'M GETTING TOO OLD FOR THIS.

I KNOW WE'VE NEVER ASKED THIS OF EACH OTHER, BUT HOW OLD ARE YOU? MY GUESS IS TWENTY-FOUR. AM I CLOSE?

I SUPPOSE THAT'S ONLY A FAIR QUESTION IF I OFFER TO TELL MY AGE. TWENTY-SEVEN. MY BROTHER TURNED THIRTY LAST WEEK, AND HIS WIFE PRESENTED HIM WITH A PAIR OF BABY NIKE TENNIS SHOES — HER WAY OF TELLING HIM SHE WAS PREGNANT. THEY'RE PRETTY EXCITED.

YOU KNOW, SOME DAYS I'D LIKE TO BAG THIS WHOLE JOUR-NALISTIC LIFESTYLE, FIND A NICE NINE-TO-FIVE POSITION AT A SMALL-TOWN NEWSPAPER, AND LET ONE OF MY COM-PETITORS WORRY ABOUT WINNING A PULITZER.

THE DEADLINE DRAWS EVER CLOSER. MUST GO.

YOURS, KC

P.S. WHAT DO YOU THINK? IS IT ABOUT TIME WE MET FACE TO FACE?

Lauren froze. She read the last line again. This is what she had been waiting for. Or so she had thought. How many times had he written that P.S. and then erased it the way she

156

had removed similar lines in her letters to him? She decided not to pause to think. As her heart pounded, her fingers tapped to the beat, typing out her response:

DEAR KC,

YES, I THINK THE TIME FOR A FACE-TO-FACE HAS COME. I'M GOING TO SOUTHERN CALIFORNIA THE FIRST WEEKEND OF AUGUST. BY ANY CHANCE COULD YOU MEET ME THERE? MAYBE WE COULD HAVE A LATE DINNER ON FRIDAY NIGHT IN LA? OR PERHAPS BRUNCH ON SUNDAY?

ALWAYS, WREN

P.S. YOU WERE CLOSE. I'LL BE TWENTY-FIVE NEXT MONTH.

Her hands felt clammy as she touched the send button. Was she doing the right thing? If they met in Los Angeles, her brother could join them for dinner. Nothing safer than that.

KC wrote back saying he would be returning from a trip to Chicago that weekend and wouldn't be able to meet her in LA. He suggested the following weekend in Oregon and asked if she would consider flying to Portland. She wrote back that her frequent-flyer miles weren't quite at the point she could travel two weekends in a row.

However, just to leave the possibility open, Lauren signed up at work for vacation time that second weekend of August and all of the third week. That way, if she did end up somehow in Portland, she could fly on to Victoria to see her parents for the week. It wasn't too impossible. But it was a little scary.

Once she knew her vacation time was cleared at work, she wrote KC that she was considering Portland after all. What did he have in mind?

KC wrote back:

DEAR WREN,

I WANT YOU TO KNOW I'M NERVOUS ABOUT OUR MEETING,
AS I'M SURE YOU ARE. HERE'S MY PLAN: I THOUGHT PER-
HAPS WE COULD GO HIKING. YOU SAID A FEW WEEKS AGO
THAT YOU HAD A GOOD TIME ON A DAY HIKE WITH YOUR
CHURCH GROUP. WELL, A BEAUTIFUL WATERFALL,
MULTNOMAH FALLS, IS LOCATED ABOUT HALF AN HOUR'S
DRIVE FROM THE PORTLAND AIRPORT. IT'S ONE OF MY
FAVORITE HIKING SPOTS, ESPECIALLY THIS TIME OF YEAR. I
THOUGHT WE COULD MEET THERE. MAYBE IT WILL MAKE
THINGS A LITTLE LESS AWKWARD IF WE WALK AS WE TALK.
AFTER THAT, IT'S UP TO YOU. I'LL LEAVE THE BALL IN YOUR
COURT. NO PRESSURE. LET ME KNOW WHAT YOU DECIDE.

YOURS, KC

Oh, but Lauren did feel pressure. Lots of pressure. For
days she worked through all the pros and cons of this plan.
It would have been safer to meet him in a more public situation, like dinner in LA with Brad. Still, she had no reason to
distrust this man. Hiking was a good idea. It would make
their first "date" casual and more relaxed for both of them.
She wrote back that she would like to think about it a little
more. KC's response left her with an even bigger dilemma:

YOU MIGHT AS WELL KNOW THAT I LIVE IN PORTLAND.
THAT'S WHY IT'S EASY FOR ME TO INVITE YOU HERE. IF
THIS AUGUST WEEKEND DOESN'T WORK OUT, LET'S NOT
STRESS OVER IT. I TRAVEL SO MUCH THAT I MIGHT BE IN
YOUR NECK OF THE WOODS EVENTUALLY.

Should she tell him where she lived? Lauren wondered. Then what? Reveal her real name? Give him her phone number? Maybe they should talk on the phone first. Just to break the ice. Somehow that didn't settle well with Lauren. She realized that part of the reason this relationship felt safe and secure was because the anonymity was a form of protection. She couldn't give that all up. Not yet, not over the phone.

In a moment of need, Lauren asked Mindy if she could come over after work. It was only a week until Teri's wedding and two weeks before Lauren might go to Portland. It was time to ask for advice.

Mindy arrived a little after seven with a grocery bag in her hand. "Mint chip and a bag of Oreos," Mindy announced, handing the bag to Lauren. "I like my cookies crushed on the bottom of the bowl. Should I help?"

"You didn't need to bring anything," Lauren said. "But thanks. Why don't you make it the way you like it and make mine the same way. Do you want anything to drink?"

"Coffee. Black."

"I hope I have some," Lauren said, checking her cupboard.

"Don't worry. I brought some coffee, too."

"Boy," Lauren said with a laugh, "this was a casual invitation, and you've gone all out. What's the occasion?"

"I'm expecting you to tell me," Mindy said with a tilt of her head. "I know something is up, Lauren. Get it out. Go ahead. Just break it to me gentle-like. You're leaving, aren't you? You have a job teaching somewhere, and you wanted to let me be the first to know."

"No, it's nothing like that."

"Whew!" Mindy expressed exaggerated relief as she

mashed the cookies in the bottom of her bowl with the back of the ice cream scoop. "So this is girls' night out, and that's it, right?"

"No, not exactly. I need some advice. I didn't want to get into it at work."

"Speak to me. I am a storehouse of opinions."

"I know."

Mindy shot her a playfully appalled look.

"It's like this," Lauren said, rinsing her rarely used coffeemaker and filling it with water. "I've sort of met someone."

"Really?" Mindy's eyebrows went up, and a cagey smile spread across her lips. "It's about time. Where did you meet him? At church? Don't tell me at Kroger's. I don't sanction relationships that begin in the fruit department. That's where most of them belong!" She looked down at Hawthorne rubbing against her leg. "Can he lick this?" She held up the ice cream scoop.

"He probably would like to, but I've put him on a diet."

"Sorry, baby. Maybe next time. Now, as you were saying...?"

"I didn't meet him at the grocery store or at church. Actually, we met more than a year ago."

Mindy dropped the scoop into the sink and spun around to give Lauren a warning look. "If you're about to tell me it's that guy from the bank picnic last year, I'm going to lose my appetite right here and now."

"No, of course not! Didn't I tell you? I heard he moved to Seattle or some place. He moved a long time ago."

Mindy slipped a coffee mug under the stream of java coming from the coffeemaker and said, "Do you have any sugar? I need sugar."

"In the cupboard by your head." Lauren picked up her ice cream bowl and headed for the couch. She felt nervous about finally telling someone, especially Mindy, about KC.

"Let's start over," Mindy said once she was settled on the easy chair with her mug of coffee and bowl of ice cream. She tilted her chin toward the vent in the ceiling and said, "Oh, that air feels good. So tell me. What's his name?"

"Well," Lauren cautiously took a bite of ice cream mixed with the smashed cookies and said with a full mouth, "This is good!"

"You're stalling."

"His name is KC."

"Casey? Casey what?"

"No, it's the initials, K.C."

"Which stand for...?" Mindy did little loops in the air with her spoon.

"I don't know."

"Okay. Let's try an easier question. How did you meet him?"

"Well, my brother sort of introduced us."

"Elaborate for me, if you don't mind."

Lauren put down her bowl of ice cream and leaned forward. She took a deep breath and spewed out, "Okay. We met on the Internet a year ago in July when my brother was here. Remember when he brought me the computer? And, well, we've sort of been corresponding all this time, and don't worry — he's a Christian. So now we both thought we'd like to see each other, and I'm considering going to Portland in two weeks to meet him at a waterfall."

Mindy's mouth dropped open. She plopped her spoon back into her bowl and stared at Lauren. "A year? You've written to this man for a year, and you never told me?" Her look of hurt was genuine.

"I couldn't tell you, Min. I didn't tell anyone. I couldn't. It's such a bizarre thing. I never guessed it would get this far. We just started writing one letter after another and before I knew it —"

"You fell in love," Mindy finished for her.

"Maybe. Yes. No. I mean, I don't know. How can I be in love with someone I've never seen?"

"You love God," Mindy answered.

"That's different."

"Not always," Mindy replied. "When one heart opens to another heart, it usually results in love."

"So what should I do?"

Nineteen

A re you asking me if you should meet this guy?" Mindy
asked.

"Yes."

"No."

"No?"

"No!" Mindy spooned a scoop of mint chip into her
mouth. "No way should you put yourself at risk like that.
Where did you say he wanted to meet you? At a waterfall?"

"Multnomah Falls. It's near the airport in Portland."

"Probably nice and remote. Just the right place for an ax-
murderer to make mince meat out of you and hide the evidence."

"Oh, Mindy, he's not like that. You know he isn't."

"No, I don't. And neither do you. Listen to me, Lauren.
There are men who work the Net regularly, luring women to
meet them, and those women never return. Don't you read
the papers?"

"I feel as if I know him, Mindy."

"Right." She snorted. "You don't even know this guy's

name!" She shook her head and took another scoop of ice cream. "You're crazy, Lauren. Crazy to even think about it. Does he know your name or where you live?"

"No."

"Good. Keep it that way."

A silence enveloped them before Mindy said, "I'm serious about this. Things happen to you, Lauren. Remember that homeless guy who stole your purse?"

"That was a fluke."

"You're too trusting! You need to realize that people in this world aren't as innocent as they used to be. You've been duped more than once. This one sounds like the biggest dupe of all. I can't believe you even considered it!"

"You wouldn't say that if you knew him the way I do."

"Oh, please!" Mindy rolled her eyes. "I just have one question for you: Since when did God need an electronic dating device to get two people together? If you're meant to be with him, you two will end up somehow, some way, meeting someday. You need to stop trying to be in control and let God be in that position."

Lauren thought long and hard about Mindy's words. There was a lot of wisdom in them. There always was, mixed in with her crazy brashness. She had trusted Mindy's common sense before and hadn't been disappointed. This was a pretty major decision. Perhaps she should take her friend's counsel to heart.

However, in some ways she felt closer to KC than she did to Mindy. Finally she e-mailed him and said she couldn't make it to Oregon that weekend. They would have to wait for the Lord to work out another meeting time and place for them. KC responded with understanding and said that since she wasn't coming, he was considering going to see his brother that weekend:

MY BROTHER TELLS ME THERE'S A CHANCE I CAN STEP IN AND TAKE OVER THE NEWSPAPER IN HIS TOWN. AN APPEALING THOUGHT. HE AND HIS WIFE INVITED ME TO SPEND THE WEEKEND WITH THEM. I COULD USE THE R & R. I GUESS OUR DIVINE ENCOUNTER WILL HAVE TO WAIT. I'M A PATIENT MAN.

YOURS, KC

Lauren considered showing the letter to Mindy. What kind of ax-murderer visits his brother and says he's willing to wait patiently for a divine encounter? She knew Mindy would say, "An exceptionally clever one." So Lauren kept the letter to herself along with the other treasures in her notebook.

The day before Lauren left for Teri's wedding, Mindy asked if she was satisfied with her decision not to meet KC.

"I can wait." Then with a smile she repeated KC's response. "I'm a patient woman." It made her feel as if she and KC had some sort of secret code. Lauren felt more connected with him than if she had disagreed with Mindy's counsel. The link to KC grew only stronger.

The next day Lauren had to work late because it was the second of the month and therefore one of their busiest times. She finally balanced her cash and dashed to the parking lot, completely flustered and certain she would miss her 6:45 flight to Burbank. Her luggage was in the car, so she could drive directly to the airport. But the Friday night traffic was atrocious, and Lauren started to lecture herself on the folly of booking a flight that she couldn't possibly make. What had she been thinking?

She pulled into the airport at 6:20 and chose the short-term parking, even though she knew she would be sorry on Sunday afternoon when she had to pay the big bucks to retrieve her car from there. If she didn't park close, she would certainly miss her plane.

With only one bag and an extra large shoulder bag to jostle, Lauren locked her car and ran into the terminal. Her bag was small enough to be considered a carry-on, and the shoulder bag qualified as a purse. No need to check luggage. She dumped them both at the security check, blitzed through the scanner, and grabbed them before they were completely out of the x-ray machine. Then, running down the corridor, she heard an announcement for the final boarding for the flight to Burbank. Dashing to the gate as the attendant was about to close the door, Lauren flashed her ticket and asked breathlessly, "Burbank?"

"Yes," the attendant said, pulling off the stub of her ticket. "You better hurry!" A few more panicked strides, and she was at the door of the plane.

"Just in time," the attendant at the door said. "We have a fairly open flight so sit anywhere you like. You'll need to switch to your assigned seat when we stop to take on more passengers."

Lauren plopped in the nearest open aisle seat and smiled politely at the disinterested man sitting in the window seat. The attendant lifted Lauren's bag into the overhead bin as Lauren tucked her "purse" under the seat. Then, catching her breath, she looked up at the seat number and then down at her ticket. Wonder of all wonders, she had landed in her assigned seat.

I guess the good Lord is watching out for me after all. I made the flight, and I'm in my seat. After... She checked her ticket and saw they had a snack on the flight, then stopped in Dallas to take on more passengers, then dinner on the way to Los Angeles, then on to Burbank. The best part about this flight was that she didn't have to change planes the whole trip. *After Dallas, I'll have some dinner, and if I get in a good nap, I'll be ready to stay up all night talking to Brad. I want to hear his opinion on KC.*

The attendant passed by, closing the overhead bins. Lauren asked him for a blanket and pillow. He handed them to her and said, "We'll be serving dinner soon. Leave your tray table up if you don't care to eat."

"That's a change in schedule, isn't it?"

"It might be. I usually don't work this flight."

"Oh. It'll be down. I'm ready to eat now!" Her lunch had consisted of a granola bar and a bottle of mineral water, her half-hearted attempt to lose weight.

"We'll serve a few minutes after take-off," he said with a gracious smile.

Lauren snuggled under the blanket and popped on the headphones, drowning out the safety instructions and flight information being repeated as the plane taxied down the runway. The engines' hum quickly lulled her into a deep sleep.

The night before, after an exhausting day at work, she had tried to pack for the trip and found she didn't have an appropriate dress that still fit her. In a flurry, she had gone to the mall and bought the first thing she found, a cool, summer dress with gold trim and a missing button. She bought it anyway and then stayed up half the night trying to fix it and decide on shoes and accessories that matched. By 2:30 that morning she had everything ready to go, including the gift-wrapped present.

Lauren suddenly opened her eyes and sat up straight. She had left the gift at home on the table. Oh, bother. Now she would have to mail it. Or maybe she could find something quickly in Escondido, if she could get to a mall before the eleven o'clock wedding.

After dinner was served, Lauren returned to her nesting position and fell into a deep, albeit uncomfortable, sleep. When the plane landed, she felt groggy and only interested in more sleep. Passengers came on. The plane took off and made a second stop. Lauren blinked and looked past the man still seated next to her and tried to look out the window at Los Angeles airport, a place she had become familiar with during her years in college. It was bright outside, which surprised her. She dozed again until the plane came to its third stop. Shuffling off with the other weary passengers, she made her way into the terminal and toward the car rental booths.

That's funny. I thought we deplaned outside the terminal here in Burbank. They've made some major changes since I was here last. This Native American motif is kind of a surprise. But what do I know? I'm not a decorator.

Standing in front of the car rental agent, she noticed again how light it still was outside. "Oh, excuse me," she said as she met him with a yawn. "It's much later according to my head. I have a reservation. It's for Lauren Phillips."

The round-faced man wore his long hair in a braid down his back and seemed unaffected by her chit-chat. He began to punch in the information on his keyboard.

"And I'll need a map. Particularly if you have one of the

San Diego area. I'm going to Escondido."

The man looked up at her without blinking. "What was your last name?"

"Phillips. P-H-I-L-L-I-P-S. Lauren. I reserved it with my Visa card, if that helps."

"It's not here."

"Are you sure? It has to be. I made the reservation two weeks ago. It was for this company, for tonight, for me, here in Burbank."

His expressionless face took on a glimmer of knowing. She had to ask. "What?"

"You're in Fairbanks."

"Alaska!?" Lauren shouted.

He didn't move.

"I'm in Alaska?" She looked around frantically. This wasn't Burbank Airport. Not even a renovated Burbank.

"Would you like a compact car or midsize?" he said.

"I don't want a car! I want to get to LA! Where's the ticket counter?"

He motioned with his eyes; his face remained stoic.

Lauren grabbed her luggage and marched off to the ticket counter where she told her story to the only agent who was working there that night. Fortunately, the woman was a perky young transplant from California and showed more compassion than the man at the car rental booth. She called for a supervisor and, as she explained for Lauren what had happened, her fingers flew over the keyboard searching for a flight to LA. The supervisor examined Lauren's ticket and listened again to Lauren say, "And I ran to the door just as she was closing it and I said, 'Burbank?' and she said, 'Yes' and took my ticket stub and told me to hurry."

"We would like to make this right for you, Ms. Phillips. Your flight to Los Angeles will be at no charge."

"I appreciate that," Lauren said, trying to calm down and think straight.

"Okay," the petite agent announced. "This is the best I can come up with. I have a flight leaving here at 8:55 in the morning. It will route you through Seattle and then to San Diego and back up to LAX."

"There's nothing tonight?"

"Nothing. The only other flight I can get seats on tomorrow before 8:55..." She punched in some more numbers. "Actually, it's wait-listed right now, but that one would take you back through Anchorage and then to Portland with a four-hour layover and then a direct flight to Burbank that afternoon arriving at —"

"I can't get there in the afternoon," Lauren said. "I have to be in Escondido for a wedding by eleven."

The supervisor and agent exchanged glances.

"There's nothing out of here that could get you to southern California before eleven tomorrow morning. I'm sorry," the supervisor said.

Lauren let out a heavy sigh and swallowed the tears of desperation that had sprung up. She looked at her ticket, at the agent, at the supervisor, and down at her luggage. "Okay. Just get me back home to Nashville and don't charge me for it."

"We'll do better than that," the supervisor said. "We'll give you a free ticket to anywhere our airline flies in the United States and treat you to a complimentary meal in our VIP lounge tonight. Why don't you come with me."

"I'll need to make a few phone calls."

"No problem. Do you like smoked salmon?"

Twenty

❧

N ow, let me get this straight," Mindy said in the lunchroom on Monday. "You ended up in Alaska and missed the wedding, but the airline gave you a free ticket. The newlyweds are having a reception somewhere in Oregon this weekend. So you're using the ticket to go to Portland on Friday, and you think God did that so you could meet KD."

"It's KC, and yes, it's possible that God is working all this out. You're the one who's always telling me he's in control."

Mindy put her head in her hands. Her body language said, *Yeah, but that's only when God doesn't have goofballs like you to work with.*

"It's still a bad idea, Lauren. Far too risky. You would be making a poor choice and counting on God to rescue you. He does expect you to use the brain he gave you, you know."

"I didn't say I was going to meet KC for sure. I'm still thinking about it. You have to admit, though, the free ticket is a little unusual."

"Not for you, Lauren," Mindy muttered.

Lauren's spirits were unquenched by her friend's sarcasm. That evening an e-mail from KC was waiting for her:

DEAR WREN,

HOW WAS YOUR TRIP TO CALIFORNIA? I GOT STUCK IN CHICAGO AND SPENT SATURDAY NIGHT AT THE AIRPORT. NOT MY FAVORITE WEEKEND PASTIME. LAST NIGHT I DID SOMETHING RATHER BRAVE, FOR ME. I TOLD MY PARENTS ABOUT YOU. THEY'RE ACTUALLY THE FIRST PEOPLE I'VE TOLD ABOUT OUR RELATIONSHIP. THEY HAD ALL KINDS OF CAUTIONS AND WERE PRETTY ASTOUNDED AT MY CONFIDENCE THAT THIS WAS A GOOD THING. THEY'VE BEEN WORRIED, OF COURSE, THAT I WORK TOO HARD AND HAVEN'T DATED ANYONE IN YEARS. PROBABLY FIVE YEARS. MAYBE MORE. I'VE BEEN SO CONSUMED WITH MY CAREER. NOW I'M DOING WHAT I ALWAYS THOUGHT I WANTED TO DO, AND YET THAT NIGHT ON THE LUMPY BENCH AT O'HARE, I KEPT THINKING ABOUT MY BROTHER AND HOW SIMPLE AND SWEET HIS LIFE SEEMS. I'M LOOKING FORWARD TO SEEING HIM THIS WEEKEND. THAT IS, UNLESS YOU'VE RECONSIDERED AND WOULD LIKE TO MEET ME AT MULTNOMAH FALLS. NO PRESSURE.

YOURS, KC

Carefully choosing her words, Lauren wrote back that she was, in fact, still considering the trip to Portland. She didn't go into any details about the free ticket or the detour to Alaska. No need to drop hints that she was a magnet for peculiar occurrences. The part about his telling his parents won her heart over. It couldn't have been clearer that he wanted to marry and settle down the way his older brother had. These were not qualities of a psycho serial killer — were they?

"That's it," she announced to Hawthorne. "I'm going to do it!"

One of the advantages of working at a bank was that she had opened a savings account and had arranged to have money automatically deducted from her paycheck each week. It was mad money that she had never touched. If this didn't qualify as a "mad" decision, then nothing she would ever do would.

She marched out the door and drove to the airport where she cashed in her free ticket. She would arrive in Portland close to noon on Friday, have time for a hike with KC, then she would drive down to Teri's little town of Glenbrooke, stay in a hotel, and spend Saturday with Teri and her new husband at their wedding reception. She would drive the three hours back to Portland on Sunday and fly up to see her parents for the week. If by any chance things went exceptionally well with KC, he could fly up to Victoria with her to meet her parents. There wasn't a figurative storm cloud in sight.

She arrived home at 8:30 and left a message with Teri's parents, informing them of her plans. They said they would pass the word on when Teri called in. She and Gordon were driving up the coast on their honeymoon and expected to be in Glenbrooke by Friday evening.

Then Lauren sent KC an e-mail note:

I MAY BE CRAZY, BUT I'M COMING TO PORTLAND. I ARRIVE FRIDAY AT NOON AND CAN MEET YOU AT THE FALLS BY ONE. SHOULD I BRING A PICNIC?

His answer didn't come through until Wednesday morning, which made her slightly stressed. She calmed as she read his words. He began with a Browning quote:

SO I SHALL SEE HER IN THREE DAYS
AND JUST ONE NIGHT, BUT NIGHTS ARE SHORT,
THEN TWO LONG HOURS, AND THIS IS MORN.
SEE HOW I COME, UNCHANGED, UNWORN!
FEEL, WHERE MY LIFE BROKE OFF FROM THINE,
HOW FRESH THE SPLINTERS KEEP AND FINE,
ONLY A TOUCH AND WE COMBINE!

YES, ROBERT AND I HAVE SHARED MANY COMMON EXPERIENCES, AND NOW HERE'S ANOTHER TO ADD TO THE LIST. SO, YOU AND I WILL MEET ON FRIDAY.

ARE YOU NERVOUS? I ADMIT I AM. I'M CONCERNED YOU MIGHT NOT LIKE WHAT YOU SEE AND MAY PREFER THE HEART OVER THE HEAD AND FRAME. I KNOW YOU WILL BE BEAUTIFUL TO ME, INSIDE AND OUT. BUT WITH A BOND LIKE OURS, APPEARANCES ARE OF LITTLE MATTER, AREN'T THEY? I KNOW I WILL BE HAPPY SIMPLY TO BE WITH YOU. I WILL KISS THE FINGERS THAT BROUGHT YOUR HEART TO MINE. I'LL BRING THE SANDWICHES, YOU BRING THE WINE. (OR, IF YOU PREFER, SOFT DRINKS. I'M A 7-UP DRINKER.) I'LL BE STANDING AT THE FIRST LOOKOUT AREA AND WEARING A BEIGE BASEBALL HAT AND A WHITE T-SHIRT. I HAVE A DARK GREEN BACKPACK WITH A BROWN LEATHER BASE. THREE MORE DAYS!

YOURS, KC

Lauren read his words again and again, swallowing them like rich, dark chocolate. The part about appearances being of little matter stuck with her. When she finally came off her cloud, she started to wonder: What if he was dog-ugly? Or only four feet tall? What if he weighed five hundred pounds? Or what if he was super skinny and frail? What if he was in a wheelchair? She doubted he would have suggested hiking if that were the case. He could be missing a limb, though. But it wasn't likely that someone who traveled constantly did so with an artificial leg or arm. Or was it?

Saving his letter and printing it out for her notebook, Lauren wondered if perhaps he was such a complete geek that no one had wanted to go out with him for the past five years. Deep inside she knew she loved him for his heart. It didn't matter what he looked like. It reminded her of *The Phantom of the Opera*. The Phantom was hideously ugly and hid behind a mask. His voice was what drew Christine to him, as well as his ability to teach her to improve her singing. However, Christine never saw the Phantom's face until the end. When she did, even though it repulsed her, she chose to love him. However, disaster awaited them. The many years of blending their voices in the dark came to a painful end. Others never understood her strange love for him.

"Have I fallen in love with a Phantom, Hawthorne? Why did I say I would meet him?" The purring cat settled himself on her lap and listened to her woes. "I could still call it off." She reread his letter. "No, I couldn't. I have to go through with this, no matter what happens. And who knows? He could be normal through and through."

At work Thursday Lauren tried to avoid eye contact with Mindy. But the all-knowing counselor had figured out that Lauren had made plans to go to Portland and continued to express concern. She left Lauren in the parking lot that evening with a dramatic hug and said, "If I never see you again, I want you to know you've been a true friend. My only consolation will be that I'll see you in heaven."

"Get out of here," Lauren said. "I'm not going to disappear."

"Will you promise me one thing?"

"I don't know. What is it?"

"Promise me you'll allow yourself an out. You know, even if you get all the way to the falls and something inside you, which will, of course, be the Holy Spirit, tells you to pull back, will you do it? Will you promise me you'll run like the wind?"

Lauren smiled. "Okay. I promise I'll run like the wind if anything inside me tells me to pull back."

That night she packed in a flurry, loading two suitcases with everything she owned that still fit her. For nearly an hour she fiddled with possible outfit combinations and finally decided on a pair of jeans instead of shorts for the big meeting the next afternoon. Her legs weren't very tan, and she didn't like any of the tops that went with her shorts. She had several T-shirts laid out on her floor but put off that decision until the morning.

Then, with her luggage lined up by the door, she checked Hawthorne's automatic cat feeder and cleaned his litter box. "I know you won't even miss me. There's enough food and water here for a week. Remember to floss after every meal, and I'm serious when I say no wild parties while I'm gone."

Hawthorne's flat "meow" was evidence enough that he would be fine.

She barely slept, tossing in bed while her mind ran an unending marathon. She felt like the description Mindy had given her a year ago of a person walking around with a big "if" over her head. What if this was a huge mistake? What if it was right, and they decided to elope right then and there? What if... The alarm clock's shrill interruption was a welcome friend.

The "ifs" didn't leave her alone, though. Not in the shower, not on the plane, not at the Portland car rental booth, and not on the freeway heading east with the unfolded map in her hand. She found Multnomah Falls with no problem and could see the 620-foot beauty from the parking lot.

She felt no qualms about moving forward. Only peace. It was a gorgeous, sunny day. That was a good sign. Lauren checked her hair and makeup and practiced a smile in her rearview mirror. Then, with a deep breath, she got out of the car, merrily closed the door, and marched off to the entrance of Multnomah Falls.

Twenty-One

֍

The time was exactly 1:00 p.m. as Lauren came up from the freeway pedestrian tunnel that led to the falls. Dozens of tourists were coming and going. The warm afternoon sun felt good on her hands, which were chilled from the car's air conditioner. She noticed an espresso cart to the right and remembered she was supposed to bring the drinks. No problem. They could pop back down here for KC's 7-Up. Behind the cart, long lines formed for the snack bar window, and behind that was a wonderful stone lodge. Lauren had read about it in a brochure at the airport while waiting to rent her car. The lodge was built in 1925 and now housed a restaurant and gift shop. Perhaps they could find a quiet table at the restaurant after their hike and...

Out of the corner of her eye, Lauren spotted a man wearing a beige baseball cap. He wore a windbreaker, so she couldn't tell what color his T-shirt was. Dark hair stuck out the sides of his cap, and he was much shorter than she had hoped he would be. Lauren hurried to catch up with him on the wide trail up to the first lookout point. "Excuse me." She could hardly contain her excitement. "KC?"

The surprised man turned around and spoke to her in Japanese. He had on a blue button-down shirt and no backpack.

"Oh, excuse me," Lauren said, slightly bowing her head in response to the tourist's gesture of nodding at her. They both nodded again, and she broke away, her cheeks fiery hot with embarrassment.

A few yards farther up the trail she reached the first lookout point. Surveying the large open area with the stone railed observation point, Lauren counted a half-dozen men wearing baseball caps. None of the caps was beige and none of the men carried a green backpack.

Lauren hung back by the trees on the side, wanting to make sure she didn't approach the wrong man again. Suddenly there was a tap on her shoulder. She jumped slightly and turned to see the Japanese man handing her his camera. By his rapid words and gestures, she figured out he wanted her to take his photo on the observation point with the falls in the background.

"Okay," she said, accepting the camera and tipping her head to the man.

He chattered his instructions, pointing at the lens cap, and walked back to where he wanted to pose for the photo. Lauren put her eye to the viewfinder. The man was close up, filling the frame and leaving no room for the waterfall. "Wow! This is quite a camera," she muttered, trying to adjust the zoom lens.

The tourist continued to point and call out his directions to her. Lauren gave the lens a twist and suddenly a green backpack and part of a beige hat appeared in the frame. Her heart began to pound faster. She moved the camera slightly and made the image smaller. Yes, he wore a white T-shirt, and the green pack over his shoulder had a brown leather bottom.

Lauren could hardly breathe as she moved the camera so she could see his head through the lens. Locks of dark brown hair peeked out from under the beige baseball cap. "Come on, turn around, turn around," she muttered.

He slowly turned. Her focus through the camera lens was perfect. A strong, chiseled jaw laid the foundation for a tender smile that pulled up the laugh lines across his cheeks and bunched them together like a collection of gold threads in the corner of his eyes.

"KC," she whispered.

Lauren moved the camera toward him and felt her cheeks flushing a tingly red. This was it. KC was standing there, big as life, as real and as wonderful — no, more real and more wonderful — than she had imagined.

Click. Her trembling finger snapped a picture — not of the tourist, but a close-up of KC.

The tourist, assuming she had taken his picture, trotted over and tried to retrieve his camera, thanking her and bowing.

"But I didn't take your picture yet," she said, holding on to the camera.

The man yanked it from her hands, a scowl spreading across his forehead. He marched off, mumbling Japanese phrases, which Lauren guessed weren't especially complimentary.

Oh yeah? Well, wait till you have your film developed!

Lauren looked up to see if KC had noticed the clamor.

He was looking in the other direction, scanning the faces of each woman who walked past him.

Suddenly Lauren couldn't move. KC was standing only twenty feet away, and she couldn't move. The only other time she remembered feeling this dumbfounded was that night in the alley when the homeless man stole her purse. An overwhelming impulse swelled inside her.

Run, Lauren. Run!

And run she did. All the way back to the parking lot where she hid in her rental car, feeling her heart pound in her ears and her eyes fill with tears.

"I can't do this!" she told herself, turning the key in the ignition. "He's too wonderful and I'm...I'm not ready for this. What if he wouldn't like me? Or if he would spend today with me and then decide he never wanted to see me again? I couldn't live with that."

Fueled by the vast emotional furnace of painful memories of abandonment, first by her father and then by Jeff, Lauren rammed the car into reverse and peeled out of the parking lot. She was mad, flaming mad, and she didn't exactly know why. As she drove, she decided the best course was to do what she had done for years: Swallow her feelings and go on. Change the subject. Move on to the next thing.

Today, the next thing happened to be getting herself to Glenbrooke. Teri had called the day before and left a message for Lauren saying there weren't any really nice hotels in Glenbrooke so arrangements had been made for Lauren to stay with Teri's friends, Jessica and Kyle. Teri had left directions and said Lauren couldn't miss their white Victorian mansion on the top of Madison Hill. Jessica would be expecting her in time for dinner.

I'll be a little early, that's all. I'll hear all about Teri's romance, and I'll meet new people, and I'll laugh and smile and have a good time. This never happened. I never should have agreed to meet him. I feel so foolish!

Maneuvering her way through a maze of Portland bridges, Lauren found the I-5 Freeway and headed south. She passed under a sign with the word "Salem" on it. She drove on, not thinking, not feeling, set on arriving in Glenbrooke with her emotions calmed. If Lauren was good at anything, it was fixing things. She would fix this weekend so it would be just right — fun, relaxing, and in every way enjoyable. The only thing she had never tried to fix was the part of her heart that bore the sign "rejection" over it. She would not allow anyone, especially another man, to pass under that sign and enter that part of her life again. In her panicked state, it made complete sense that she had done the right thing to turn from KC before he could reject her.

It was all a fairy tale, a fabricated relationship through a computer screen. None of it was real. Mindy was right. I never should have agreed to meet him.

Then Lauren remembered something else Mindy had said about how God didn't need an electronic dating device to get two people together. If she and KC were meant to be together, they would end up somehow, some way, meeting someday.

Was that supposed to happen, God? Was that our divine encounter, and I just blew it? I couldn't go through with it. Did I do the right thing?

There was no answer as the car sped down the freeway toward Eugene.

"It's awfully quiet in here," Lauren said aloud, her quavering voice echoing off the ceiling of the rental car. "What's going on, God? Are you about to abandon me, too?"

Twenty-Two

With one hand on the steering wheel and the written instructions to Kyle and Jessica's home in the other, Lauren turned right on to Main Street in Glenbrooke and glanced out the top of her windshield. There it was: Madison Hill. And nestled in its emerald crown stood a great white jewel of a mansion.

"Wow, Teri wasn't kidding! I hope these people aren't eccentric weirdoes like my Great Aunt Clarita. This could be a nightmare weekend."

Pulling into the long, circular driveway, Lauren slowly approached the front of the Victorian charmer. A wide porch wrapped around the whole house, and lining the base of the porch were dozens of the most gorgeous hydrangea bushes Lauren had ever seen. The yard seemed to go on and on behind the house with a rolling green lawn and huge friendly old trees. A swing hung from an apple tree to the right. Off to the left swung a large, empty hammock, inviting Lauren to come sink into its knotted embrace.

Lauren pursed her lips and swallowed the last bit of her

wracked emotions. She would not, absolutely would not, allow her emotions to ruin this weekend. She was here to celebrate with Teri. Even if the owners of this estate turned out to be exotic nut cases, she would be cordial and as supportive of Teri as Teri had always been of her.

Closing her car door and lifting her sunglasses, Lauren called out, "Hello? Anyone home?"

Two golden retrievers came bounding toward her from around the side of the house. Lauren walked up the wide steps, lined with terra cotta pots bubbling over with bright summer flowers. The dogs followed, two steps behind. She stopped by the open front door and patted the friendly pooches on the head.

"Hello?" She knocked on the wood frame and heard the clip, clip, clip of heels on the hardwood floor. An older woman appeared. Her silver-rimmed glasses matched her silver-white hair. She was wearing a huge white Shasta daisy pinned to the bodice of her dress. With quick strokes, she wiped her hands on her checkered apron.

"Come in, come in!" she said, holding open the screen door. "I'm Ida, Ida Dane. You must be Lauren. Teri told us to expect you."

Lauren stepped inside. Ida shooed the dogs away and closed the door.

The entryway was breathtakingly beautiful, yet warm and welcoming. A spiral stairway was the focal point. But Lauren took in each detail of the entry, enjoying the gleaming hardwood floors, the large oak hall tree to the right with etched, beveled glass, and the huge ceiling light fixture with frosted glass bells hanging down like dainty flowers. Bunches of fresh flowers greeted her from the antique entry table to the left. French doors opened to a charming parlor with a marble-hearthed fireplace and inviting, overstuffed chairs. Lauren noticed that the fabric covers on the furniture in the parlor were the same as her rose floral couch and easy chair covers. She instantly felt at home.

"You're early, you know. We didn't expect you until this evening. No matter. We're preparing a few things for the reception tomorrow. I understand you and Teri were room-mates in college, is that right?"

Lauren could barely answer yes before Ida plunged on. "She's an absolute favorite of everyone's here. We all missed her terribly when she moved to Maui at the beginning of the summer. Have you met her husband?"

"No."

"I understand he's Austrian," she said in a lowered voice. "Can you imagine? I shouldn't wonder if he doesn't honor us with a bit of yodeling at the party tomorrow. Teri tells us he's quite an individual. And Teri being a Spanish teacher and all. It's an international experience for us here in Glenbrooke, if you catch my meaning. The pity is that they're going to live in Hawaii. You know, don't you, that he's a minister? Just like her father. Shall we go into the kitchen?"

Lauren nodded and followed, amazed that Ida finally took a breath. This woman definitely bore a resemblance to Lauren's Great Aunt Clarita.

"That's always the way, isn't it?" Ida continued. "We marry a man just like our father."

The image that struck Lauren was that of her biological father rather than of Stan. With great effort, she stifled the thought that she might end up with a man who would aban-don her, a man who could be homeless at this very moment, stealing purses from innocent women. She would never be a victim again. Hadn't she proved that today? How could she ever trust a man? Even Jeff, who had seemed so stable and predictable, had abandoned her.

"Look who's here!" Ida announced as they stepped into the high-ceilinged, freshly painted, and renovated kitchen.

A woman about Lauren's height, but slimmer, stood at the sink peeling carrots. On the counter was a pile of fresh carrots and a bowlful of snap beans. The woman's long, honey-blond hair was pulled back and fastened with a twisted red bandanna. Behind her a tall, broad shouldered man with thick, dark hair stood with his arms wrapped around her middle. He appeared to be patting her stomach and whispering sweet nothings in her ear. Startled by Ida's announcement they turned around, embarrassed. Both said "Hi" at the same time.

The man moved toward Lauren first. "I'm Kyle," he said extending a huge hand. His handshake was tender, his eyes clear green, and his jaw firm. "Glad you could come, Lauren. Teri will be happy to see you."

The woman wiped her hands on a towel and slid in next to Kyle. She had a simple, honest face with moss green eyes and fair skin. The scar above her lip curled up when she smiled. But what made the deepest impression on Lauren wasn't the woman's appearance, but the calm gentleness that seemed to float around her. She offered her cool, small hand, and Kyle said, "This is my wife, Jess." He slipped his arm around her shoulder.

"Will you listen to us!" Ida said. "So busy making introductions all around we haven't asked if Lauren would like something to drink. It's a hot afternoon, and I'll bet a glass of lemonade sounds good to you about now."

Now Ida reminded Lauren of some of the sweet ladies from Shelbyville, who loved to use their southern hospitality on Lauren whenever she paid them a visit.

"Yes, lemonade would be nice, thank you." She felt hot in her jeans and wished she had worn shorts instead.

"I'll get it for us," Kyle offered. "Ice?"

"Sure. This is a beautiful home," Lauren said, glancing at the hanging copper pots above the island cook-top range. The deluxe kitchen opened into a breakfast nook where a thick, round oak table sat in a bay window area. Ferns hung in front of the window, and a blue pitcher stuffed with white Shasta daisies graced the center of the table.

"Thanks," Jessica answered shyly. "We still have a lot of work to do."

Lauren had assumed this was Ida's home. But did it belong to Kyle and Jessica? Could such a young couple own a place like this? She guessed them to be in their late twenties. Kyle might be thirty. Perhaps Ida was his or Jessica's mother; although Lauren failed to see any resemblance to either of them.

Kyle offered Lauren the lemonade and asked if she wanted to settle into her room. She followed him past the breakfast nook into a hallway that led to a laundry room.

"What do you do, Kyle?" she asked, hoping for a clue as to who ran this place.

"I'm a paramedic. Jessica teaches English at the high school. That's where she and Teri became such good friends. I knew Teri before that, from church. We worked with the youth group together."

They walked past several closed doors. "Unfinished projects," Kyle explained, nodding toward the silent rooms. At the end of the hall he opened the door to Lauren's guest room and said, "This one's fit for company."

The huge room was not only fit for company, but it also could have won an award for best bed and breakfast. Along the back wall was a bay window with a built-in window seat. It was covered with bright geranium cushions and pillows, and a matching ruffle swung across the top of the window. Outside lay yards of fresh cut grass and a picture-perfect view of a flower garden in full bloom. Beyond that was the beckoning hammock. A small fireplace was nestled in the bedroom's corner, and a king-sized bed was made up in fresh summer colors that matched the geranium window seat. An antique trunk stood guard at the foot of the bed. On the bedside table was a fresh bouquet of white daisies and red geraniums.

"This is beautiful," Lauren said.

"Most women say that."

"Oh? And what do the men say?"

"Not much. We don't let them stay in this room. This is Jessica's garden room. The great northwest room is directly above you."

Lauren smiled. "Let me guess: Forest green, solid oak bookshelves, four-poster bed, a larger-than-life television, and an ice box."

"You've seen it?" Kyle teased.

"Guess I don't need to. Are Teri and Gordon staying in the manly room?"

"No, we have another room upstairs all ready for them. Sort of a middle-of-the-road version. Feel free to take a look if you want. You're the first one here. The other guests should be arriving tonight. Actually," Kyle hesitated and looked over his shoulder. Lowering his voice, he asked, "Did Teri say anything to you about Kenton?"

Lauren shook her head.

Kyle shuffled his large frame and said, "Jess thought I should warn you."

"What? Is Kenton the psycho uncle who lives in the attic?"

Kyle laughed. "Almost. He's my brother. He's coming this weekend, and Teri thought we should, you know, sort of fix you two up. But Jessica is too tenderhearted to let anyone get trapped into something like that."

"And what's wrong with your brother?"

"There's nothing wrong with him. Well, not really. He and I are different, that's all. He's the studious brain boy who spends more time with computers than with people."

"Sounds like my brother," Lauren said. "Don't worry. I know how to handle that particular species. By any chance does he shower more than once a month?"

"He's not that bad," Kyle said with a laugh.

"Thanks for the warning," Lauren said, feeling a little disappointed. If Kyle had a clone somewhere in this world, Lauren wouldn't have minded falling in love with him. It would solve the KC problem and provide affirmation for Mindy's theory that if God had someone wonderful for Lauren, they would come together through natural, unforced events.

But then, what did Lauren know about God and his wonderful plan for her life? At the moment, he didn't seem to be speaking to her. And she wasn't interested in falling in love with anyone. Probably because she already had. And, try as she might, she couldn't turn this love off like a faucet.

CHAPTER

Twenty-Three

◦❧◦

After Kyle brought in her suitcase, Lauren began to hang up her clothes. She heard a gentle tap on the door. "Come in."

Jessica entered, bringing a peacefulness with her. "I wanted to see if I could bring you anything."

"No, I'm fine. This is a beautiful room. Do you guys run a bed and breakfast here?"

"No," Jessica said with a smile. "Although sometimes it feels like it. Ida thinks we should but..." She trailed off. "I want it to be home for us and that's all."

"Does Ida live here?" Lauren wasn't sure if she was being too nosy. But Jessica had an openness that overpowered Lauren's shyness.

"No, she's just a dear woman who loves being involved in our lives. Her husband passed away last spring. She misses him terribly. She's kind of adopted us since her son and his wife moved away almost a year ago. We're her family now."

Lauren was still curious to know where the money came from to keep up this house. She didn't think paramedics or teachers made that much, especially in a small town.

"Speaking of family," Jessica said, lowering herself onto the edge of Lauren's bed and looking as if she were about to reveal a big secret, "I wanted to tell you that Kyle's brother is coming and —"

Lauren held up a hand to stop Jessica. "Your adorable husband already warned me. Don't worry. The last thing in the world I'm interested in is starting a relationship with anyone."

Jessica nodded. When Lauren didn't offer any more information, Jessica said, "That's exactly how I felt when I came to Glenbrooke. I pushed Kyle away so many times. I can't believe he didn't give up on me."

Lauren leaned against the high-backed chair by the fire. She didn't feel free to offer any of the details of her life as Jessica had.

Jessica continued, "A lot of issues in me needed to be settled before I was ready for any kind of relationship. I had unresolved hurts over my mother and, well…, a lot of other things." She paused.

Lauren ventured a stab at this open-hearted communication. "Your mother didn't happen to leave you, did she?"

"Yes. When I was eight."

"My dad left before I was three." The words slipped out of Lauren's mouth. "My mom remarried right away."

"My dad never did. He had lots of girlfriends, I'm sure, but he never quite got over my mom's death."

"She died? That's different from being abandoned." Lauren didn't feel they were talking about the same thing after all. "People can choose to leave. They don't choose when they're going to die. There's a huge difference."

"Not when you're eight," Jessica said. "All I know is that I held in my feelings for too many years. I blamed God, and I wasn't able to move forward until I surrendered my life to him. My past, present, and future. I can't believe how much changed for me when I finally started to trust God. I mean, really trust him."

Lauren noticed that Jessica's cheeks were beginning to blush. She looked down at her sandals and said, "I can't believe I'm telling you all this."

"That's okay," Lauren said. "I think I need to hear it."

There was a pause. Lauren felt compelled, for some reason, to pour out her heart to this woman. Within twenty minutes, without planning any of it, Lauren had spilled the saga of Jeff and KC, and leaving KC at the falls. It was so unlike her. But something about Jessica and this house, this room, melted her defenses and made her feel peaceful and safe.

With a sigh, Lauren concluded, "Now I'm the one who can't believe she's telling you all this. I didn't mean to dump on you."

"I don't mind a bit. In a lot of ways, I know what you feel."

Again, a small pause surrounded them. The pause didn't carry the weight of embarrassment with it. It was a reflective moment of shared, silent wonder, a moment filled with the richness of commonly held truth.

"Isn't it peculiar," Jessica said, "that the very thing you have been so hurt by is what you end up doing to someone else?"

"Excuse me?" Lauren felt her defenses go up.

"Your deepest hurts came from being abandoned and

feeling the rejection of that. Now, without even thinking about it, you abandoned KC, and I would imagine he feels rejected."

Lauren felt her defenses leave her body like a flock of frightened geese. She heard herself whisper, "You're right."

"I'm sure you weren't thinking of that at the time. You were dealing with a life of hurt in that one moment. I would have done the same thing, if I were you."

"I left him," Lauren said, still dazed by the realization. "I'm a deserter."

"You were a frightened woman acting on instinct. Do you want to hear what I did?" Jessica asked. "I ran away from home. Not as a rebellious teenager; I was twenty-five. I came here, to Glenbrooke, and tried to change my identity. All I wanted was to run so far away from my father that he would never find me."

"What happened?"

Jessica smiled, and the scar on her top lip curled. "My heavenly Father found me, and he sent Kyle to rescue me."

Just then a heavy knock sounded on the closed door.

"Come in."

"What are you girls doing?" Kyle asked, poking his head in.

"Talking about boys," Jessica teased. "Go away!"

"Sorry! I didn't see the 'No boys allowed' sign."

"I'm only kidding. You can come in," Jessica said. "I heard the phone ring a while ago. Who was it?"

"My dear, misguided brother. He's not coming after all."

"Oh, that's too bad," Jessica said. "Did he give a reason?"

"Life. It stinks. That's all he said."

"So sorry I'm going to miss making his acquaintance,"

Lauren mumbled sarcastically.

"I like her," Kyle said to Jessica, tipping his head toward Lauren. "Let's keep her around."

Jessica turned to Lauren and with a straight face said, "Why don't you move to Glenbrooke?"

"Wouldn't I love to! This place is like the town time forgot. I've always wanted to live in a small town. By any chance do you know if your school is in need of another English teacher?"

Jessica looked surprised. "I thought Teri said you worked at a bank."

"I do now. I just received my credential a month ago."

Kyle and Jessica exchanged glances. "Really?" Kyle said. "How coincidental." He reached over and gave his wife's shoulder a squeeze. "It just so happens our one high school, which has one English teacher, might very well be looking for someone to fill that position this fall."

"Really?"

Before Kyle could answer, a car horn blared. Out the window Lauren could see the two golden retrievers racing for the front of the house.

"They're here!" Jessica said jumping up from the bed. "Come on, Lauren. Teri's going to be so glad to see you."

They reached the front porch at the same moment that Teri and Gordon did, accompanied by the two jumping dogs. Squeals of delight and loud hellos echoed off the porch ceiling. Hugs and kisses were delivered all around. Gordon was the loudest and most affectionate of them all — with the people and the dogs. The minute Lauren heard him speak, she knew he was Australian, not Austrian. She repressed a giggle, thinking of how dear Ida had expected a man in lederhosen to yodel for her. Although, the way this man was the instant life of the party, Lauren didn't doubt that he could yodel with the best of them.

"Lauren," Teri cried, giving her a huge hug and a kiss on the cheek. "I almost didn't recognize you! Look at your hair. You look wonderful!"

Teri was the one who looked wonderful. The glow of a new bride made her flawless skin radiate, and her wide smile lit up her whole face. She still wore her long, wavy brown hair wild and free, cascading down her back. Today it was clipped up on top of her head. A few renegade tendrils played chase across her temples in the afternoon breeze.

"Let me help you with that," Kyle said, reaching for Teri's shoulder bag.

A wry smile crept up Gordon's face as he said in his charming accent, "There's a lot more where that came from, mate. We seem to have arrived with a car full of the stuff."

Teri rolled her eyes and said confidentially to Lauren and Jessica, "His idea of traveling light is a pair of swim trunks and a toothpick."

"I heard that, Mrs. Allistar."

A look of glee spread across Teri's face as she met Jessica's gentle gaze and mouthed the words, "Mrs. Allistar!"

"Let me see your ring," Jessica said.

Teri held out her smooth, tanned hand bearing a simple wide band of gold. "We match," she said, reaching for Gordon's hand and showing them his identical gold band.

Lauren remembered that Teri never wore jewelry. It had been one of Lauren and Teri's biggest differences in college. Lauren was going through a "beads and bangles" phase and never left their room without wearing at least half a dozen pieces of jewelry. Teri, on the other hand, was a purist and would tease Lauren about the way she could hear Lauren coming down the dorm hallway.

"She tried to get me to wear mine through my nose, but I wouldn't have it," Gordon said.

Everyone laughed and began to unload the luggage. They formed a line, carrying the bags up the magnificent staircase.

"Guess what I brought you, Kyle?" Teri asked.

"Tamales?"

"No, but it's almost as good. Six jars of my grandmother's salsa."

"Did you hear that, Jess? I'm in heaven."

"Right," said Gordon, having a look around the spacious mansion. "I believe this is my heavenly reward, but where are all the angels?"

"I'm right behind you," Teri said, following him up to the last step.

Gordon reached the top of the staircase, put down his suitcase, and as Teri cleared the top step, he scooped her up in his arms and said, "Which way to the honeymoon suite for me and my angel?"

Teri started to laugh and playfully pound his back with her fists. "I keep telling you, Gordo, you only had to carry me over the threshold the first night." As she said it, Gordon's foot became tangled in the hallway runner, and the two of them went toppling to the floor. The other three ran to help them. The couple were laughing so hard they couldn't speak.

Teri caught her breath first. "Every night of our honeymoon," she said, as she wiped the sparkling tears from her eyes, "he's tried carrying me to the room. So far we've only made it over the threshold once without a disaster." She rubbed her shoulder. "Will one of you please tell him that's enough so he'll stop? He won't listen to me."

"What's that you say, dear?" Gordon asked playfully.

"It's a requirement for all men to go partially deaf the moment they say 'I do,'" Kyle said, pulling back instinctively before Jessica could swat at him.

Teri hopped up, laughing, and offered Gordon a hand. "This one was half deaf when I married him."

"Old surfing accident," Gordon said, pointing to his right ear. "It was at the finals. Perhaps you saw it on the tellie. About nineteen years ago. The board caught the underside of a wave and curled up like this." He used his hands to demonstrate. "Flipped out the side and came down on me, like —"

Teri joined him and in unison they said, "A hammer pounding a nail through a piece of paper."

"Oh, oh," Jessica said. "Sure sign of married life. You can already finish each other's stories!"

Lauren had put down the bag she was carrying and slowly made her way down the stairs while the two couples became involved in their married-life banter. It had suddenly become too much for her. They were married. They were happy. She was miles and miles away from them and their lives. Jessica's words kept pounding in her head, "You abandoned KC. I would imagine he feels rejected."

Quietly slipping into her garden guest room, Lauren closed the door and retreated to the inviting window seat. Staring out at the vivid garden, Jessica's words echoed again and again, "You abandoned KC. You abandoned KC."

"I did, didn't I?" she whispered into the silent air.

Running her fingers along the edge of the window sill, she felt forlorn. The one thing she thought she would never do, she had done. And she had done it to the one person who held more of her heart than anyone ever had, or possibly ever would. Once she had written to KC:

I HOPE YOU FEEL IN ME THE SAME KIND OF SAFE PLACE I HAVE COME TO KNOW IN YOU. I HAVE NEVER BEEN SO CONNECTED WITH ANYONE IN MY LIFE. I'M AFRAID THAT IF OUR RELATIONSHIP EVER CEASED, I WOULD GO BACK TO BEING HALF A PERSON, AND I DON'T WANT TO LIVE LIKE THAT AGAIN. YOU MAKE ME THINK. YOU GIVE MY DREAMS FERTILE SOIL IN WHICH TO TAKE ROOT AND GROW. MAY GOD PROTECT US BOTH FROM EARTHQUAKE, FIRE, OR FLOODING OF THE SOUL.

The disaster she had feared had come. And she had been the harbinger.

Twenty-Four

In the midst of Lauren's brooding, Jessica knocked on the door and spoke softly, "We have some dinner ready if you're hungry."

"Okay, thanks. I'll be there in a minute." She was still sitting on the window seat, holding a fluffy pillow tight around her stomach. For the past hour Lauren had tried to cry but couldn't, tried to sleep but couldn't, tried to dream up an easy out but couldn't. A lot of life-core issues were staring her in the face, and she couldn't turn away. She could no longer "stuff it," as Mindy had accused her of doing so many times.

She found her way into the kitchen, where Jessica was grabbing a bottle of salad dressing from the refrigerator. "We're eating outside," she said. "I didn't know if I should disturb you. Were you getting in a little nap?"

"Not really. Just thinking."

An expression of concern covered Jessica's face. Her body language said, *I know. I understand.* All she verbalized was, "If you ever want someone to sit by you while you do your thinking, I invite you to call on me. I used to do my best thinking at the cemetery, all alone. But I know some people are better at thinking when they have a user-friendly shadow."

"Thanks. I might take you up on your offer. Can I help with anything?"

"No, everything is out there: fresh veggies from our garden and a big salad, and Kyle has some chicken going on the barbecue."

Lauren followed her out the back door on to a large wooden deck. Three round tables with big canvas umbrellas were positioned across the deck like a European sidewalk cafe. Kyle stood over a huge, built-in brick grill, a long pair of tongs in his hand. Gordon and Teri flanked his sides, offering cooking suggestions.

It was a beautiful August evening. Turquoise blue skies, swept clear by the summer breeze, faded into dusk and then to night. They sat around the table talking until the stars came out. Most of the conversation was about Teri and Gordon's wedding until Teri asked why Lauren hadn't been able to come at the last minute. She felt so at ease with these four that she told them her disaster of ending up in Fairbanks. They all laughed, even Lauren.

Thoughts of KC wouldn't go away. When they finally started to clear the table and go inside, Lauren drew up the courage to ask Kyle if he had a computer.

"Yes. And you might be interested to know I got it from my brother."

"My brother gave me mine, too," Lauren said. She wasn't sure how to ask if she could borrow his computer to send an e-mail letter. Not that she knew yet what she would say to KC. But she needed to know that, if she thought of something, she could send it to him before she went home to Nashville.

"You want to see it?" Kyle asked.

"Sure." She followed him through the elegantly decorated parlor and into a dark library with bookshelves to the ceiling. He went over to the impressive mahogany desk, snapped on the green banker's lamp, and lowered himself into a tuck-and-roll burgundy leather chair. Kyle showed her his laptop while rattling off some of the facts about his particular model, which meant nothing to her.

"I mostly use it for e-mail," he said.

"Me, too," Lauren agreed. She still didn't know how to ask if she could use it. Maybe tomorrow, after she had composed a letter in her mind. "This is a fabulous office," she said, looking around. One book caught her eye. She walked behind the desk and had a closer look. "May I look at this?"

"Sure. That's Jessie's. She collects antique books."

"Really? I do, too."

"Then you two should talk. She would love to tell you about them. Every book has a different story about where she bought it. I think most of the ones on that shelf she picked up at Oxford."

"England?"

"She went to school there."

"Really? Your wife is an amazing woman."

"You don't have to tell me," Kyle said with a proud grin.

One of the inset lights in the ceiling suddenly flashed and went out. Kyle went over to the library ladder on wheels and rolled it to the side of the tall bookshelf where the light was located. "I should have guessed this one was about to go," he said, climbing up toward the light. "I just changed the one next to it last week." He was on the third rung when the phone rang. He kept climbing as it rang again.

"Can you grab that Lauren? Everyone else is probably outside."

"Hello?" she said, thinking she should have answered with "The Buchanan Estate" or something impressive.

"Hi, Jessie," a male voice said. "It's me. Is your big ugly gorilla home?"

"Uh, just a minute." She covered the mouthpiece and said to Kyle, "It's some guy who wants to know if a big ugly gorilla is home."

"That's Kenton. Tell him he's a bum for not coming."

Lauren hesitated.

"Go ahead. Tell him."

"Um, Kyle says you're a bum for not coming."

"Oh yeah? Well tell him he's a bum for not calling me back like he said he would."

"He says you're a bum for not calling him back."

Kyle took out the bulb and shook it by his ear, verifying that it was burned out. "Well, you tell him if he wanted to talk to me he should have done it in person."

She didn't have the receiver covered that time.

Kenton said, "I heard, I heard. Tell Freddy the Fireman…" He paused and then said, "Why can't he come to the phone so I can tell him myself?"

Feeling part of the conversation now, Lauren said, "He's up a ladder at the moment."

Kenton started to laugh. "That's sounds about right. Is there a cat in a tree or something?"

"No, he's changing a light bulb. I may need to call 911 if he electrocutes himself," she said, watching Kyle balance at the top of the ladder.

"This isn't Jessica, is it?" Kenton asked.

"Ah, no. I'm a house guest."

"Oh. You must be the one they were going to try and fix me up with."

His words halted her.

Kenton's voice took on a serious tone as he said, "Look, I'm sure you're a wonderful person, and you sound like you're a lot of fun and everything, but I'm kind of in a complicated relationship right now, and this whole fixing us up thing wasn't my idea. That's part of the reason I didn't come, if I can be honest with you."

She couldn't answer.

"I hope I didn't hurt you with what I just said. I didn't mean to. I don't know what they told you about me. But, well…," he stammered. "I'm…ah, I'm not looking to start anything, and I thought that maybe they thought I should be."

Lauren still had no response. All she could think was that a complete stranger was rejecting her over the phone.

"Are you still there? Ah, what was your name?"

"Lauren," she articulated, suddenly finding her voice. "My name is Lauren, and if you're going to be so arrogant and rude to a person over the phone, you should at least know her name!" She hung up the phone with a bang.

Kyle had descended and stood still before the desk with a look of wonder on his face. Then, tucking the light bulb under one arm, he slowly began to applaud.

Lauren slumped into the chair and buried her face in her hands. "I'm sorry."

"No need to apologize. You gave him exactly what he needed and exactly what he deserved. And that is why I applaud you." He kept clapping.

"No, don't," Lauren said, looking up and holding out her hands, motioning him to stop. "I don't like what I just did. I'm sure he was trying to be as considerate as he could. I overreacted."

The phone rang.

"I think you had better answer it this time," Lauren said, excusing herself and returning to the kitchen.

Jessica stood over the dishwasher, pouring in the detergent.

"Can I do anything to help?" Lauren asked.

"It's all done."

"Where are Gordon and Teri?"

"They went for a walk. How are you doing?"

"Well, for starters, I yelled at your brother-in-law over the phone and hung up on him."

"You did?" Jessica's eyes grew wide as Lauren explained what had happened. "He's really a nice person," Jessica said. "I like him a lot. I'm sure he was trying to be considerate of your feelings even though it came out in an awkward way. He's usually very articulate."

"He was articulate, all right. The problem was me. I felt he was rejecting me, and I couldn't handle it. I mean, the guy doesn't even know me, and he was rejecting me."

"I can see how you might feel that way," Jessica said. "I wonder..." Her thoughts trailed off.

"What?"

"Well, I was thinking about what we were talking about this afternoon. It seems that the thing we resent happening to us becomes the thing we end up doing to someone else, unless we face our own pain head on and stop the cycle of hurt."

"Or the hurt runs you over," Lauren said.

"That can happen. But I don't think it has to." Jessica reached over to the window sill above the kitchen sink and picked up a stack of cards. "These are the promises I go back to. They're what keep me from being run over, I guess."

"May I see them?" Lauren flipped through the handwritten verses on the cards.

The first one read, "I will never leave you nor forsake you. Hebrews 13:5." And the others: "I have called you by your name, you are mine. Isaiah 43:1." "Wait for the Lord; be strong and take heart and wait for the Lord. Psalm 27:14." "The Lord has been mindful of us; he will bless us. Psalm 115:12." "When my father and my mother forsake me, then the Lord will take care of me. Psalm 27:10."

"I keep a few in my purse and a few by our bed," Jessica said. "Whenever I start to feel overwhelmed, I find a piece of God's Word to cling to. I never thought of it this way before, but these are sort of like safety air bags for me. Sometimes I do get hit head-on with past hurts, but these verses keep me from being destroyed. I still get bumped around, but I'm not demolished."

Lauren didn't know if she had ever admired anyone as much as she admired Jessica at this moment. "That's a great idea."

"On a couple of them, I wrote on the back what the verse means to me. Here." She reached for the top card, flipped it over, and read aloud, "God, my heavenly Father, has promised that he will never leave me, or ignore me, or pretend I don't exist. Even if no one else ever loves me or cares about me, God does."

Lauren smiled.

"And this one," Jessica flipped to the next card with the verse, "I have called you by your name, you are mine." She turned it over and read her paraphrased promise. "Every single time you play Red Rover, Red Rover, I will call out your name, Jessica. I will call out, 'Red Rover, Red Rover, send Jessica right over!' I will always do this because I want you on my team every time we play."

Lauren felt a lump in her throat. Jessica smiled and handed her the stack of cards. "Would you like these?"

"I couldn't take them. They're yours," Lauren said.

"I don't mind sharing."

"Maybe I could copy down the verses and think through for myself what the promises mean."

"Some index cards are in the top drawer over there," Jessica said. "Please feel free."

"Thanks," Lauren said. "I do feel free here."

Kyle entered the kitchen and said, "Lauren, would you mind picking up the phone? Kenton wants to talk to you."

She gave Jessica a glance, let out her breath, and said, "Okay."

"There's a phone here, or if you would like you can use the one in the library."

"This one's fine." She picked up the phone and said, "Before you say anything, I'd like to apologize for overreacting. I'm sorry."

He seemed caught off guard. "Hey, I was the one who was out of line. I apologize."

"Don't worry about it. It's okay."

"You sure?"

"I'm sure."

"Well, good night then," Kenton said.

"Good night." She hung up the phone and turned around. Kyle and Jessica had slipped out of the kitchen. In the quietness she could hear Gordon and Teri's laughter floating in from the swing on the front porch.

She picked up the stack of verse cards she had left on the counter and read through them once again. They all reflected a loving, patient, and kind God who wanted to have a close relationship with her.

She thought of how KC had said he was a patient man. Would her deserting him at Multnomah Falls have a fatal effect on his long-suffering?

Twenty-Five

Teri and Gordon's wedding reception began at noon on Saturday and lasted far into the night. It seemed to Lauren that every Glenbrooke resident came, and each of them brought a gift. Teri and Gordon spent more than two hours seated in a white wicker love seat under a shady elm tree opening the gifts. Each item seemed to have been selected as a special expression of love for the couple. Lauren met dozens of warm, wonderful people, including a Mr. McGregor who was the school principal. He said he would be delighted to keep Lauren's resume on file in case they ever needed another English teacher.

Teri had said at dinner the night before that she loved Maui and couldn't wait to return there with Gordon, but at the same time, a part of her would always remain here, in Glenbrooke. Now Lauren knew why. The people of this town loved Teri, and they had no problem showing an equal amount of love for Gordon. He comfortably rolled through the day, taking everything in stride. Lauren could see why Teri loved him and why they were so good for each other.

Sometime during the evening Kyle started a campfire in a pit out back in a wide clearing. A group of teens from the youth group had gathered around the fire to roast marshmallows and sing. Lauren felt compelled to join them even though she wasn't a teen. Something about the words they sang drew her to the group; the thoughts were so pure and right. She felt a spiritual responsiveness stir inside her that she hadn't experienced since her high school days.

At the same time, she felt remorse, and that drove her to be alone. She found sanctuary in her garden bedroom with the window open, watching this night of celebration. She imagined no one could see her sitting there in the dark.

The night sounds floated up to her shelter. Little children shouted and chased the dogs, a few babies slept in their mothers' arms, and the adults pulled up chairs in circles like a modern-day version of a wagon train. She could hear one of the older men telling a story about the day they opened the first gas station in Glenbrooke. A few "tweener" boys were arguing in their yet-to-mature voices over who was cheating at a game of Ping- Pong that Kyle had set up on the deck. Several women chatted as they busied themselves with the task of helping Ida organize Gordon and Teri's gifts. Laughter and music floated across the top of this hill where everything that was sacred to Lauren seemed to have happily settled.

For more than an hour she sat and watched, listened, and thought. By ten-thirty most of the guests had said their farewells. Lauren felt somewhat recharged, even though she had no more answers than when she had retreated to the bedroom. The tender ache of regret still hung over her. She knew she couldn't do anything about KC now, but she could help in the kitchen and get her mind off herself.

She found Ida alone in the kitchen, boxing up a large piece of the cake in a white pastry box. Lauren picked up a dish towel and began to dry the remaining plates in the dish drainer.

"We kept ours in my uncle's freezer and ate it on our one-year wedding anniversary," Ida said, tying the box with a blue ribbon. "He was a butcher, you know. My uncle. Not everyone had freezers in those days. Young people today don't hold to the old traditions any more. They need someone who has been through life to teach them, don't you think?"

"I know Jessica and Kyle are glad to have you," Lauren said.

"Well, the poor dears. She has no family to speak of. Her mother died when she was only a child and her father… Can you imagine his cutting her off like that? He hasn't contacted her once. Didn't even come to their wedding."

"I didn't know," Lauren said. Apparently not only had Jessica's mom died, but it also sounded as if her father had abandoned her, which made Jessica's personalized verses from the night before even more meaningful.

"He had a great affluence over her, you know." Ida raised an eyebrow.

Lauren wasn't quite sure what to make of that comment. This was the same woman who had told her Gordon was from Austria. Perhaps Jessica's father had been among the influential founding fathers of Glenbrooke, hence the grand old house.

She was about to politely probe when Jessica stepped into the kitchen and said, "There you are, Lauren." Kyle, Gordon, and Teri followed right behind her. "May we see you in the library? There's something we would like to ask you."

"Oh, oh. I'm in trouble now," Lauren said, handing her wet dish towel to Ida.

"Here's the anniversary cake I told you about," Ida said to Teri. "Now you put this in the freezer right away so it will stay nice and fresh."

Teri obliged while Lauren followed the others into the library. Kyle shut the doors before beginning the mysterious meeting. She felt as if they were enacting the final chapter of a Gothic novel.

"I didn't do it, whatever it was," Lauren said.

Jessica glanced at the others and then said, "We wanted to ask you a couple of questions. Please don't feel put on the spot. Teri told me you were planning to leave tomorrow to visit your parents in Canada."

"Yes. They live in Victoria."

"Well, feel free to turn this down, but we were wondering —"

Just then Teri opened the door and joined them. "What did she say?"

"We haven't asked her yet," Jessica said.

"Just tell her," Teri said and then plunged ahead and did so. "Do you want to go to Hawaii with us tomorrow?"

Lauren laughed. "Sure! Why not?"

"We're serious," Teri said.

"You see," Jessica explained, "Kyle and I were planning to go to the islands with these guys and spend a few days together. We thought Kyle's brother was going with us; so we made reservations for five. Since he has backed out, we have an extra plane ticket and room reservation. I hope this doesn't come across as rude as it's beginning to sound, but we all thought it would be fun if you came with us."

"Of course it doesn't sound rude. How could a free trip to Hawaii sound rude? I'd love to go. I can see my parents any time, but I've never been to Hawaii. Will you let me pay for the ticket?"

"There's no need. It's already taken care of. All you have to do is come." Jessica looked at Kyle and added, "We wanted to tell all of you something else."

Kyle slipped his arm around Jessica's shoulders and said, "This is our big announcement for the three of you. We're going to have a baby."

Teri let out a shriek, sprang from her chair, and rushed to hug them both in one encompassing embrace. "Why didn't you say anything before?!"

"This was your day," Kyle said as Gordon gave him a hearty handshake. "We didn't want to steal anything from your celebration. Our guests will be glad to return for another party when the baby comes, but today was for you."

Lauren smiled and offered her warm congratulations to both of them.

"There's more," Kyle said, looking at Lauren.

"What? Twins?" Teri asked.

"Not that we know of," Kyle said, raining a smile of affection on his wife. "Jess won't be returning to teach in the fall, which means we just so happen to be in need of a high school English teacher." He looked at Lauren. "Do you know anyone we could recommend for the position?"

"Wait a minute," Lauren said. "Will somebody pinch me? I know this is a dream. First, will you go to Hawaii; then, will you teach in Glenbrooke? This can't be happening."

"Why are you asking Lauren to teach English?" Teri asked. "I thought she was an art major?"

"I was my sophomore year. That didn't last. I guess we didn't talk about it, Teri, but I have my teaching credential. I graduated as an English lit major."

"That's perfect!" Teri agreed. "You'll love living here. I sure did."

"You're welcome to stay with us as long as you want," Jessica offered. "We can help you find a place, too, if you like."

Lauren thought about how wonderful it would be to live in the garden room, at least for a while. "I'll be glad to pay rent," she said. "Especially if you need the extra income since you won't be working."

Teri burst out laughing.

Jessica said gently, "That's okay. I really appreciate your offer, but we'll be fine. We'd love for you to be our guest."

Gordon was yawning and trying hard to stay awake.

"We have an early start in the morning," Kyle said, giving them a quick rundown on the travel itinerary. He concluded with, "So it might help if we have everything packed tonight."

"Teri, do you still want us to ship the gifts to Maui after we get back?" Jessica asked.

"I think that would be the easiest. I might even leave an extra suitcase or two with things I don't need right away, if you wouldn't mind shipping them as well."

"We would be glad to," Kyle said. "You had better get your man to bed. He's about to fall asleep on us here."

Gordon's yawn at that moment was so huge Lauren felt sleepy watching him.

"That's what I get for marrying an old man," Teri teased. "Come on, honey. The party's over." She took his arm and helped him out of his chair. Gordon shuffled beside her until they reached the doorway and then all of a sudden scooped her up in his arms and successfully carried her over the threshold.

"Aha!" Gordon shouted triumphantly. "I knew I could do it." He put Teri down gracefully, and she pretended to pound his chest. Gordon looked over his shoulder and in a droll voice told his audience, "I can't keep the woman off! She's absolutely crazy about me."

"One of us is loco," Teri agreed. Then, wrapping her arms around her husband, she planted a big smacking kiss on his lips and said, "And I love him just the way he is." They headed upstairs, whispering to each other, leaving a sprinkling of invisible love dust in their wake.

Jessica said she needed to check on Ida to see if she had gone home yet. Lauren asked Kyle if she could borrow the phone and then realized she would be better off calling her parents from the airport tomorrow since it was so late.

"I was going to show you this book last night," Kyle said, pointing to a fat volume on the desk, "since you said you like old books. This is my only contribution to Jessica's collection."

Lauren examined the blue, hardback book, which was written in some kind of Aramaic looking language and opened backwards, like a Hebrew Bible she had seen once. "What is it?"

"See if you can guess."

On the front cover was a picture of a frail man looking up with a huge sack slung over his back. The copyright inside appeared to be 1904, although the numbers were the only thing Lauren could read. An inscription read, "For my favorite 'Pilgrim': May all your progress lead you safe to the arms of Jesus. Forever, Lindsey."

"Pilgrim's Progress," Lauren said with an appreciative smile. "What a treasure! Doesn't it always make you wonder who the person was when you read an inscription?"

"Lindsey was my fiancée," Kyle answered.

Lauren looked up, startled. "Oh."

"She's in heaven," he explained.

"Oh, I'm sorry. I didn't mean to...," Lauren said, closing the book and placing it carefully on the edge of the desk.

"To what? Bring back a memory of someone who's gone? It's okay. Just because I once loved another woman doesn't make my love for Jessica any less. Nor am I embarrassed by my past love."

Lauren wondered if she wasn't somewhat embarrassed that she had loved Jeff. After all, she had tried more than once to convince herself that what went on between them wasn't really love. Somehow, Kyle's words freed her. She didn't have to apologize for having loved Jeff. She had loved him. But that didn't mean she couldn't go on now and love another man. The burning question was whether KC could still love her.

"May I ask you a question?" Lauren said.

"Sure," Kyle answered.

"Jessica told me she wasn't very responsive to you when you first met."

A slow smile spread across Kyle's lips. "You could say that."

"Well, what if she had done something that hurt you horribly. Would you have been able to forgive her and still love her?"

"We had our ups and downs, that's for sure. I believe the main, and perhaps the only reason we ended up together, was because God worked everything out. See, it's my belief that if two people are both seeking God's best and if they are meant to be together, then nothing — and I mean nothing — can stop them from ending up together."

"I hope that's true," Lauren said.

"I should tell you, though," Kyle said leaning forward, "I also believe the reverse is true. If two people are seeking the Lord and if they aren't his best for each other, then nothing they try will keep them together."

"I know that's true," Lauren said.

Kyle smiled. He shook his head and said, "I wish my brother could have met you. He needs someone open and level-headed with a big heart like you.'"

"Actually, someone is in my life already. We have a few things to work out. I did something without thinking through the consequences. But I'm not ready to give up on the relationship yet. I don't know if he is or not."

Kyle gave her a brotherly, sideways hug and said, "Keep trusting God. It will turn out the way it's supposed to."

≈≫

The trip to Hawaii began early the next morning. It seemed like a dream to Lauren, even after they had landed in Honolulu and caught a connecting flight to the island of Lana'i. She sat by the window and was captivated by the azure Pacific below, dotted with white sailboats and tiny white caps on the rippling waves. They flew over beautiful, long, green Moloka'i with Maui to their left. Bubbles of excitement rose inside Lauren as they landed at the Lana'i hilltop airstrip among pineapple fields. She tried to maintain the same cool, calm demeanor as the other four and not let on that this was her first such adventure.

A Polynesian woman in a flowered muumuu greeted them as they deplaned. "Mr. and Mrs. Buchanan?" she asked. When Kyle acknowledged that was he and Jessica, the woman placed a purple orchid and white tuberose lei around his neck and kissed him on both cheeks. "Enjoy your stay on our island," she said and turned to present Jessica, Gordon, Teri, and Lauren with leis and kisses. "The van is waiting for you out front. Aloha."

"Is this like *Fantasy Island* or what?" Lauren whispered to Teri.

"No, this is like Lana'i. You don't get this kind of treatment on Maui. Ah, but Maui has the same warm, sweet trade winds." She tucked her hand in Gordon's and said, "We're home, honey."

After gathering their luggage and loading it into the van, the group headed past the pineapple fields where vast rows of green spiny shoots reached heavenward. A long driveway led them past towering Norfolk pines to the front of a huge lodge tucked in the highlands of Lana'i. Koele Lodge had the look of an English country manor. A wide porch circled the entire building, and painted on the triangle overhang that canopied the entrance was a giant pineapple. It made a lovely first impression.

"This is beautiful," Lauren said, unable to contain her enthusiasm any longer as the van stopped and the driver helped her out. A bellhop appeared at her side and offered to take her bag. "Sure. Thanks." She followed the others into the elegant lobby to register. A gigantic bouquet of bird of paradise, anthurium, and wild ginger greeted them. "Have all of you been here before?"

"We have," Jessica said, casting a smile at Kyle.

"Not us," said Teri. "I've never been on this island. Have you, Gordo?"

"Only in my dreams," he answered. "And only with you." He gave his wife a kiss.

Lauren wondered if she would be able to stand an entire week around these honeymooning mushpots. Certainly the options for activities on such an island would be limitless. She could rent a jeep and explore if all they wanted to do was lounge around. It would give her a chance to think through how she was going to explain everything to KC.

It took only a few minutes to register, and then they followed Kyle down the hallway, past an intriguing game room and gift shop, out some double doors, and down the long veranda to an adjacent building. All along the breezeway were wicker chairs with footstools that silently invited guests to stop and sit for a while. In each chair was a patchwork pillow, each sewn with a different Hawaiian quilting design.

In the adjacent building, Kyle led them to a group of four suites and handed out room key cards.

"So what does everyone feel like doing?" Kyle asked.

"I'm hitting the pool," Teri said.

"I'm with the lady in the swimsuit," Gordon said.

"A swim sounds great," Lauren agreed.

"Okay. Ten minutes then? The pool is out that way. We'll see you guys there."

Lauren slipped her key in and out of the door lock, letting the bellhop bring in her luggage. The large, airy bedroom was decorated in an inviting blue and ginger pattern and had a four-poster bed. A door led out to the front veranda. It was by far the nicest hotel room she had ever been in. "Thanks," she said, tipping the young man in the white coat. As soon as he left, she flopped onto the bed and drew in a deep breath of her wonderful surroundings. "This is where I want to come for my honeymoon."

On the table was a carafe of fresh pineapple cider tucked in ice. She poured herself a glass and read the note from the hotel's general manager. He invited her to savor her Koele moment and stated that he hoped her stay would be "an unforgettable moment of Old Lana'i hospitality." She had no doubt her stay would be unforgettable as she downed the refreshing beverage. Within minutes she was in her bathing suit and on her way to the pool.

Gordon and Teri were already there, snuggle-swimming in the shallow end. A pool attendant greeted Lauren and offered to lay out a towel for her. He spread two fluffy white towels on the lounge next to Teri's and asked if Lauren would like something to drink.

"No, thanks. I'm fine." She stretched out and surrendered to the intense sun pouring over her skin, soothing her every pore. The attendant returned a few minutes later to lay out towels for Jessica.

"Come on in!" Gordon called. "The water's wet."

"I like to get hot first," Jessica said. "What a perfect day!"

"I know," Lauren murmured back. She cracked one eye open and noticed Jessica was alone. "Where's Kyle?"

"He went to check on a tee time."

"Do they serve tea here?"

"Yes, at four. In the music room. But actually, Kyle went to check on a tee time for golf."

"Oh," Lauren said.

Before she had a chance to be embarrassed about her fumble, Gordon lifted himself to the edge of the pool and said, "Did you say tea, Jess? I haven't gone to tea in a long time."

"I'll go with you," Jessica said. "You want to come, Lauren?"

"Sure."

"I'll stay here and bake," Teri said, getting out of the pool and patting her face dry with the thick towel.

"Tea time is one of the fine things in life Teri hasn't gotten used to yet," Gordon said. "We made a deal. I'll eat her tamales if she'll have tea and cakes with me once a week."

"And tell them how many times we've had tea in the past week," Teri said, wadding up her towel and tossing it at Gordon.

"Only twice."

"Right. So I'm a week ahead. Feel free to go without me."

Lauren had forgotten what a no-frills woman Teri was. Pure, simple, and straightforward. She wished she could be that way more often. So much of her life was spent evaluating her words before speaking them and analyzing her every action. Lauren turned from conflict and fled; Teri hit it head-on.

I wish I'd faced KC head-on last Friday. I wish I'd walked right up to him, looked him in the eye, and said, "I'm Wren. Kiss me." Of course she would never really do that.

"We're on for nine tomorrow morning," Kyle said, joining the group and slipping off his shoes. "I hope you're ready for the game of your life, Gordon, because when it comes to golf, I provide some pretty stiff competition."

"Sorry to spoil your fun, but I don't golf," Gordon said.

Kyle looked shocked. "You're kidding, right?"

"No. I'm what my loving wife here calls, 'athletically challenged.'"

"Don't look at me," Jessica said to Kyle. "Do you like golf, Lauren?"

"I don't know. I've never tried to play," she said, thinking of how KC had told her his two sports were volleyball and golf. Ever since then she had wanted to give it a whirl.

"Great!" Kyle said, pulling off his shirt. "We're on for tomorrow morning at nine."

"Well, we're going to tea now. Would you like to come with us?" Jessica asked Kyle.

He handed her a tube of sunscreen and sat on the edge of her lounger waiting for her to cover his back with the stuff. "That's okay, Jess. You ladies go have yourselves a tea party, and Gordo and I will hold down the fort here at poolside."

"Gordon's going with us," Jessica said.

"What are you doing to me, buddy? You don't golf, but you take the ladies to tea? You trying to score some points here?"

"We all gotta do what we do," Gordon said with a wry grin. "I do tea; my wife doesn't. She'll keep you company."

"Great," Kyle said. "I just happen to have my portable backgammon game here. As I recall, you have yet to beat me at this game, Teri."

"Think back, oh small-brained one," Teri teased. "It just so happens that on our first missions trip to Mexico I took you on twice, whipping you both times."

"I demand a rematch," Kyle said, setting up the board on the table next to Teri's cabana.

"We're going, dear," Jessica said, playfully kissing her hubby on the neck. "Play fair."

"I always do."

Gordon offered one arm to Lauren and the other to Jessica. "Ta-ta," he called over his shoulder. "We civilized folk will leave you to your competition."

"I think Kyle's idea of a dream vacation is one competitive event after another with lots of food delivered between matches," Jessica said quietly as they walked away. She didn't sound mean about it. Lauren observed that these two loving couples had their own areas of interest which they obviously pursued without offending their mate. She wanted a relationship like that.

"We should wear something kind of nice," Jessica suggested. "I can be ready in fifteen minutes."

"Let's meet in the lobby, then," Gordon suggested.

It took Lauren closer to twenty minutes to change clothes. Gordon and Jessica were waiting for her. As the threesome entered the music room, sweet chords from a harp rolled past them. The music floated around the small tables and chairs upholstered with mint-colored fabric and made of rich koa wood. The small round tables were grouped in fours for close conversations for the dozen or so hotel guests who were already there. On the walls hung a variety of antique instruments, including lutes, mandolins, and many Lauren didn't recognize. In the center of the room, hanging from the ceiling, which was painted with pineapples and palm fronds, hung an exquisite light fixture with bunches of glass fruit hanging from its many elegant arms. Lauren spotted an amber pear, light purple grapes, and red apples.

To the side of the room, a long tea cart and buffet were set with three-tiered trays, layered with delicate triangle cucumber sandwiches, ladyfingers, petit fours, and an assortment of cakes and breads.

Lauren went first in line and filled her individual silver teapot with steaming water. She glanced through the packets of tea in the basket and then asked the attendant, "Do you happen to have any Irish Breakfast tea?"

"I'll check in the kitchen," she said and noiselessly slipped out. Lauren went ahead and selected her goodies, placing them on a china plate. She wove her way between the tables to an empty one in the corner and sat down, waiting for Jessica and Gordon. The attendant entered and with a white gloved hand offered Lauren two Irish Breakfast tea bags on a glass plate.

"Will madam be staying with us long?"

"Just until the end of the week," Lauren said, not accustomed to such service.

"I'll make sure we have your choice of tea each day this week."

Just then a loud clatter broke the subdued sounds of tea time. Lauren watched as Gordon, who apparently had collided with the tea cart, stumbled to catch his balance. With a thunderous crash and a gangly swoop of Gordon's arms, the tea cart toppled over.

Everything spilled but a flying slice of sponge cake which Gordon somehow managed to catch with his saucer. The room fell silent with all eyes on a red-faced Jessica and Gordon. He held up the undamaged slice of cake as if it were a trophy.

"Light as a feather, these!" he said.

Twenty-Seven

❧

D on't tell me. I don't want to know," Teri said, pretending to stop up her ears at the dinner table that evening. They dined in formal attire, which was required at the hotel restaurant.

"Let's just say I won't be taking tea tomorrow. Or ever again in this fine establishment. Although, I must say, I've done worse," Gordon said, the candlelight reflecting in his dancing eyes.

"I know," Teri groaned, turning her head to look at her husband. Lauren watched as intense, pure love shot from the eyes of her old college roommate and connected with Gordon's gaze. The love between them was electric. It amazed Lauren. She had never seen this in Teri before.

"Did you tell them about your first baptism?" Teri asked, her eyes still glued on Gordon.

"You mean when I tripped and took you into the surf with me?"

"We definitely want to hear about that," Lauren said.

"No, I mean when you baptized Kai and Jena."

"Oh, that one," he said, closing his eyes and lowering his head, shaking it slightly.

"I wasn't there," Teri said, facing the others, "but Gordon and another pastor on Maui baptized and married this couple on the same day. Gordo was about to baptize Kai, and he said, 'In the name of the Father and of the Son and of the Holy Ghost, drink ye all of it.'"

"You didn't!" Jessica said.

"Got my sacraments a bit jumbled. Turned out all right. They're still married, at least."

"Here's to married life," Teri said, spontaneously lifting her glass in a toast.

"Here, here!" They all agreed. Lauren lifted her glass of mineral water and joined the toast, even though she felt out of place doing so.

"And here's to Lauren's future husband," Kyle added. "Whoever and wherever he may be."

"Amen!" said Teri.

The glasses clinked once again. "You can't say we didn't try to fix you up with Kenton," Teri said. Then with a wink to Jessica she added, "He and Kyle are nothing alike. Kenton's the good looking one."

"I've had the unique pleasure of making Kenton's acquaintance, thank you," Lauren said.

"She called him arrogant and rude and hung up on him," Kyle said.

"When was all this?"

"The other night at the house."

Gordon reached over and gave Lauren's arm a compassionate squeeze. "Teri did worse than that to me. She slammed the door in my face, and all I was doing was bringing her a pizza."

"I did not slam the door! And you didn't bring me that pizza; I paid for it. You just happened to be the delivery boy."

Lauren started to laugh. "You married the pizza man!"

No one else caught the humor of the situation. The server cleared their salad plates as Lauren explained. "It's sort of a joke Hawthorne and I have that if God has someone out there for me, he'll have to bring that someone to my door. That pretty much limits it to a pizza man."

"Who's Hawthorne?" Teri said, still not catching anything funny about Lauren's story.

"My kitten."

"Oh, you have a kitten! Did you hear that, honey?" Teri said, turning to Gordon and taking his hand. "A little kitten. That's what we need."

Gordon turned stone-faced. "Next subject, please, if you don't mind."

Lauren felt like coming to Gordon's aid in discouraging Teri by describing the way Hawthorne had turned into a big, fat, lazy blob-cat. But she still loved him dearly, so she chose not to bash him.

Kyle changed the subject. "I almost forgot. I changed our golf game to the day after tomorrow so we could have an earlier tee-off and play the Challenge at Manele course rather than the Experience at Koele. Is that okay with you?"

"Sure," Lauren said. "You know, I was thinking maybe I'd rent a jeep tomorrow and do some exploring."

"That sounds good to me, too," Teri said.

"I'm with the lady in the safari hat," Gordon said.

"I could go by myself, if you guys want to take it easy," Lauren volunteered. "I don't want you to feel as if you have to entertain me or keep me company."

"Why don't we do this," Kyle said. "We'll keep the morning free to do whatever we want, then at noon we'll take a couple of jeeps and picnic over on Turtle Beach."

"That sounds perfect," Jessica said, leaning back in her chair. "I'm finding that mornings aren't my best time of day."

Their main courses arrived, and over candlelight and crisp, white linen, Lauren savored the best fish she had ever tasted. Everything seemed to be the best. The dessert was the best chocolate mousse she had ever had. The Kona coffee was the best coffee she had ever had. The night's sleep was the best she remembered having in a long time. And the primrose blue sky that greeted her the next morning was the best sky she had ever seen. Everything was perfect; everything but the unresolved problem with KC.

Lauren dressed and ate by herself in the dining room, staring out the window at the still, pure blue lake and woods beyond. Early morning guests walked and rode bikes along the trails that zigzagged the green resort grounds. She decided to join them and took off walking after breakfast. The birds that called from the immense eucalyptus trees were like none she had ever heard before. Fragrant flowers lined the path, and at the end of one of the trails, hidden from view of the main lodge, was a white gazebo surrounded by shrubs and jungle-sized greenery. Lauren ducked under the extensive lattice-work roof, feeling as if she had found a secret hideaway.

No one came near the gazebo. No one saw her or heard her. No one but God. And she knew he was there. She didn't know how she knew; she just did. The place brimmed with his presence. She thought of KC's experience at the chapel in London where he knew God was with him, guiding his future and granting him peace.

Lauren didn't have peace. She had remorse, deep pity for

herself, her life, her mistakes. Uninvited, great tears welled up in her eyes and cascaded down her cheeks. She felt nearly overwhelmed. "What?" she whispered to God in the shrouded gazebo. "What do you want?"

Lauren.

She held her breath. Had a voice just said her name? Or had she imaged it? One of Jessica's verses came to her mind, the one about God calling us by name because we are his. Was that it? Had God just called her name? Red rover, red rover...

All she knew was that she felt wanted more than she ever had in her life. Her heart felt strangely calmed, and she believed, really, truly believed, that God wanted her. The realization was powerful. She had known since her earliest Sunday school years that God loved her. Somehow she had never coupled that truth with this new reality: God didn't just love her; he desired her. God wanted her. He promised to never leave her or ignore her or act as if he didn't know her.

Lauren brushed away the tears and thought how only God had done what others had failed to do in her life, and what she had failed to do in KC's life. God never had run away.

It all seemed so clear to her: God faced the pain of sin head-on, and he broke the destructive cycle, just as Jessica had described it a few days ago. Lauren knew the destructive cycle of rejection. She needed to stop running and stop ignoring the pain of abandonment and feeling of unwanted-ness that she had lived with all these years. God wanted her. She needed to believe that with her whole heart.

"I do," she whispered into the quiet gazebo. Her tiny

words echoed off the ceiling. "I believe you want me," she said raising her voice.

It had been so long since Lauren had felt any love for God. She had given her heart to Jesus when she was young and had grown the most during her high-school years. Now she actually felt her heart filling with love for God. It had been so long, and it felt so good. "I really want you, too, Father God. I want to fall in love with you. I want to believe all your promises to me. I want you."

With her whispered prayer came the realization that she had been going through the motions of being a believer, of loving God and following Christ, for a long time. But her heart had been surrounded by protective bars of steel put there to keep out the hurt. Instead, they had only kept in the hurt, leaving little room for love to grow.

Sometime later Lauren returned to her room, feeling as if she had been on a long journey and had just returned. No one else knew how politely "cordial" she had been to God all these years. But she was back now — free to love him, herself, and others. The tears continued to stream down her cheeks. She didn't care. They had been stored up inside her from all the hurts she had "swallowed" for too long.

She grabbed the box of tissues in the bathroom and searched every drawer in the room until she found what she wanted. A Gideon Bible. Retreating to her private front porch with her Kleenex and Bible, Lauren slipped into the padded wicker chair and began to read the Song of Solomon. It seemed like a good place to read for someone who had just returned to her first love.

Twenty-Eight

At 12:15 the group took off in two red Jeeps and headed for the other side of the island with their picnic lunch. Lauren rode in the back of Kyle and Jessica's Jeep with her sunglasses, hiding her red and swollen eyes. She felt cleansed inside and eager to contact KC to try to make things right. Yet at the same time, she felt open and willing to accept whatever God had planned for her future.

The bumpy road and constant wind didn't allow for much conversation below a shout. Lauren was content to take in the scenery and enjoy the experience. The dirt road took them through an open-field cattle ranch where the herd had the right of way crossing the road. The terrain grew more rough, and they came into an area that resembled a lost planet of prehistoric nomads.

"Are we in Bedrock?" Lauren asked as Kyle slowed down, driving more cautiously over the curves and bumps. "Isn't that Fred and Wilma's rock house over there?"

"Isn't this place eerie?" Jessica asked, holding her stomach. "They call it the Garden of the Gods."

As far as the eye could see, they were surrounded by nothing but dirt and thousands of boulders, which were all shapes, sizes, and configurations. All along the road were piles of stones stacked three or more high. The colors in this volcanic junkyard were all the same: burnt sienna. The road went on and on. All they could see was what appeared to be the ruins of a lost civilization.

"What do all these stacked rocks mean?" Lauren asked.

"That this area is 'kapu.' Off limits. No trespassing. Sacred places are on all the islands where the piled rocks indicate sacred ground."

"Why would this be sacred?"

"I think this was an ancient battleground, wasn't it Kyle?"

"I don't remember. I also don't remember the road being this long before," Kyle said.

"Or this bumpy," Jessica chimed in.

"Of course, you weren't pregnant last time. How are you doing?"

"Okay. Not great. Lauren, can you reach the drinks back there? If you can, I'd like one of the bottles of water."

Lauren found the drinks and joined Jessica in quenching her thirst.

Trees and a clearing were up ahead. For the last mile or so they had been traveling downhill. Now the ocean was in view, with a beach loaded with sugar-white sand between them and the churning blue waves. It was a welcome sight and a vivid contrast to the desolation.

Gordo was the first one in the water. With a warrior's whoop he threw himself into the salty playground and rode the first wave that came to him like a carefree dolphin. Lauren felt that free inside. She gave into her childlike joy and joined Teri, running hand in hand into the water, laughing and splashing. As far as they could see up and down the beach, no one was in view for miles. The warm water, the warm sun, the warm friendships, and the warm Cokes all added up to Lauren knowing she would never forget this day. It couldn't get any better.

Several fishermen showed up in the late afternoon, casting their lines into the water and anchoring their long poles in the packed sand. Lauren filled her shorts pockets with exquisite shells of all shapes and colors. She walked along the beach with Teri and Jessica and told them about her intimate encounter with God in the gazebo that morning. Both women smiled their affirmation.

They drove back in the early evening. This time Lauren rode with Gordon and Teri. They were nearly to the hotel, tired, sunburned, wind-blown, and content, when Lauren decided to ask Teri something that had been driving her in loony little circles ever since she had arrived in Hawaii.

"May I ask one question?" she said. "Who's paying for all this?"

"Kyle and Jessica," Teri answered.

"I don't understand. Where did the money come from to vacation like this? And their home is incredible. Did they win the Oregon lottery or something?"

Teri and Gordon exchanged glances.

"Just tell her," Teri said. "It makes it easier."

"I'm not sure that's what Jessica wants," Gordon said. They had arrived back at the lodge, and Gordon pulled up behind Kyle and Jessica's Jeep and cut the motor.

"I'll tell her," Teri spouted. "Jessica is a multimillionaire. There."

Lauren glanced over Teri's head and caught Jessica's gaze. She had heard what Teri said, and her cheeks were turning deep red. Before Kyle or Jessica could respond, the attendant opened Teri's door, and she climbed out with Lauren right behind her.

What should I say? Lauren thought. *This is so awkward.*

Before she could think of a reasonable response, her eyes caught sight of a green backpack with a leather base. It was slung over the arm of a man who stood at the lodge's front entrance. He emerged from the shadow of the grand veranda and came down the steps. "Hey!" he called out. "It took you long enough, you big hairy gorilla!"

The world seemed to stop for Lauren. It was KC. Her hand flew to her mouth. Her eyes stopped blinking.

"Kenton!" Jessica called out. "I thought you weren't coming."

Kenton? Kenton is KC? KC is Kenton?

With no warning, all the blood in Lauren's body seemed to flush through a hole in the bottom of her feet, and she passed out, dead cold, in front of the five-star hotel.

Twenty-Nine

❦

The next thing Lauren remembered were dozens — or was it hundreds — of people standing over her saying, "Are you okay?" "Somebody get her some water." "Stand back. Let me have a look at her." She recognized one of the voices as Kyle's.

"I'm okay," she tried to say. But her lips had turned to Jell-O, and her statement sounded like, "Ahmahke."

"What's she saying? It sounded Hawaiian. Does she speak Hawaiian?"

"Lauren, try to look at me," Kyle said. "That's good. No, don't move. Lie still."

"Here's some water," the bellman said, handing a glass to Kyle.

"Nice and slow," Kyle said, lifting the glass to her lips. She sipped some and felt her head beginning to clear. His fingers were on the pulse points on her neck.

"I'm so sorry," she managed to say as the feeling returned to her lips.

"No problem," Kyle said. "You're probably dehydrated. It

could happen to anyone. Would you like to try to sit up?"

Lauren still felt wobbly, although her intense embarrassment overrode any and all other feelings. All she wanted to do was run and hide from KC, or Kenton, or whatever his name was. No, she didn't want to hide; she wanted to run into his arms and feel his embrace surrounding her as she had dreamed so many times.

"Okay," Kyle said. "Let's take it nice and slow and get you standing up."

Lauren felt another pair of hands take hold of her left arm. It was KC. She was so close to being in his arms. However, all he knew about her was that she was the woman who'd called him arrogant and rude on the phone before hanging up on him.

Teri came alongside her and took Kenton's place by wrapping her strong arm around Lauren's middle. "Why don't you and I go on in? We'll leave the men to retrieve the junk out of the cars. You should drink some more water."

"I'm fine. Really."

Teri kept holding her up as they ascended the steps and entered the lobby. Quietly, when they were out of range of the others, Teri said, "I'm sorry I told you like that."

"Told me what?"

"About Jessica being a multimillionaire. I know how you feel. I almost fainted, too, when I first found out. They don't act like it at all, so after a while you forget. Do you want to sit down?"

"Sure."

Teri led her to a plush, pillow-lined couch in the spacious lobby. The high-beamed ceiling opened to a second floor with a beautiful polished wood railing. On the wall in front of them was a gigantic, natural stone fireplace.

Jessica joined them and sat in a broad chair with a footstool, both upholstered in a rich gold and burnt orange brocade. She suddenly seemed like a queen to Lauren. "Are you okay?" Jessica asked quietly.

"Yes. I'm so sorry to embarrass you the way I did."

"Don't say that. You can't help it if you fainted."

"No, I mean —"

"I'm the one who said it so loud," Teri said. "Sorry, Jess."

"Oh," she said, the blush returning to her cheeks. "It's okay. Really. Let's order something for you to drink, Lauren." She motioned to the hotel staff person who was walking by with a silver tray in his hand. "May we have two iced teas?" Jessica asked. "That's for Kyle and myself. What would you and Gordon like, Teri?"

"Two ginger ales," Teri ordered. "One with a lime twist."

"I'd just like water," Lauren said.

He was about to walk away when Jessica said, "I suppose we should order something for Kenton."

"He likes 7-UP," Lauren blurted out before she could stop herself.

Teri and Jessica turned and stared at her.

"I mean, I'd like 7-UP instead of water. That's what I was trying to say."

"Make that two 7-UPs," Jessica said. "I think Kenton does like 7-UP."

The server left them. Lauren felt her heart pounding so loudly she was sure the other two women could hear it. She closed her eyes and drew in a deep breath.

I can't believe this is happening! I must look awful. My bathing suit is filled with sand, the pockets of these shorts are filled with shells, this shirt is filthy, I'm sunburned and sweaty, and my hair must look atrocious! I can't believe this is how KC sees me for the first time.

She opened her eyes, and there he stood, directly before her, leaning down to eye level. It was like looking at him through the viewfinder of the camera all over again: the firm jaw; closed-lip smile; laugh lines gathered up at the corner of his eyes; broad forehead; and dark brown hair. Only this time he was scrutinizing her features.

"How are you doing?" he asked softly. Or was it cautiously? The way an innocent man would approach a woman who had bitten off his head over the phone at their last encounter. He removed his baseball cap, as if being respectful, and ran his hand through his straight hair. Lauren couldn't take her eyes off his strong hands. Those fingers had typed beautiful words to her, words that linked their souls and melted their hearts together. And now, here they were, only a few feet away from each other, and she couldn't make a single sound come from her constricted throat.

The server arrived with the beverages and handed a 7-UP to Kenton. "Is this for me?"

"Yes," Jessica said. "Is 7-UP okay?"

"Perfect. Thanks, Jess." He sat down in a chair directly across from the speechless Lauren.

"Actually, it was Lauren's suggestion," Jessica said.

Slowly, Kenton lifted the glass to his lips. Even more slowly, he allowed his gaze to rest on Lauren.

Teri reached over and punched Kenton in the arm. "So, how ya' been? You better have a good excuse for not coming to our reception."

"I do," he said.

"Would you like to share it with the rest of the class?" Teri said in her teacher's voice.

"No."

"Your turn," Teri said, turning to Jessica. "My interrogation skills are slipping."

"I didn't think you were going to come to Hawaii," Jessica said softly to her brother-in-law. "Kyle told me about the other offer on the newspaper. I'm sorry it didn't work out. That would have been a perfect situation for you, and Kyle and I would have loved having you in Glenbrooke."

Kenton looked down at his glass and swished the ice cubes around. "Actually," he said without looking up, "the buyer who was in first position for the paper pulled out. I closed the deal this morning and decided to put some of my accumulated vacation days to good use and celebrate my new career." He looked up, glancing only briefly at Lauren, and letting his gaze rest on Jessica. "Looks like I'll be invading your restful burg by the end of September."

"That's wonderful!" Jessica said, rising and going over to the chair where he sat and giving him a hug and a kiss on the cheek. "I'm so excited for you."

Lauren couldn't help but notice how shy Kenton was. Or was it humility? He had obviously chosen to leave a prestigious journalism position and had bought a small town newspaper where he would be the editor-in-chief and probably the only staff writer. This is what he had been talking about. And now he was moving to Glenbrooke.

"Congratulations," Teri said. "You made a good choice. And guess who else is moving to Glenbrooke?"

Kenton sipped his soda, his eyebrows answering Teri that he had no idea.

"Lauren." Teri coyly looked at Lauren and then back at Kenton. "It looks as if she'll start teaching at Glenbrooke High this fall."

Kenton returned his gaze to Lauren, nodded his congratulations, then immediately looked away and wouldn't look at her again.

Kyle and Gordon stepped into the lobby. Their wives handed them their drinks.

"How long have you been here?" Kyle asked, standing beside Kenton's chair.

Kenton rose and checked his watch. He did it with such a smooth, man-of-the-world fluid motion that the simple gesture nearly took Lauren's breath away. These were the common, everyday habits she had longed to know about him. She knew inside his head by heart. Now she could meet the flesh and blood part of KC.

"Only about forty minutes. By the way, bro, I bought the paper. I'm moving to Glenbrooke next month."

Kyle's expression showed how pleased he was. He spontaneously embraced his younger brother, and the two men briefly slapped each other on the back. Now that they stood side by side, Lauren could see the resemblance, mostly in the build and the way they carried themselves. Their jaws were identical, and they both had the same high forehead. She found it impossible to stop staring at Kenton. He still hadn't looked back at her.

"Anyone else hungry?" Gordon asked.

"I am," Teri said, followed by a round of agreement from the others.

"I made reservations here for us at 7:30. That gives us an hour. Think you can hold out that long, Gordon?"

"Not a problem."

"We can always raid the little refrigerator in our room," Teri said. "I'm ready for a shower."

One of Gordon's mischievous grins appeared on his face as he said, "I'm with the woman in the shower."

"Gordo!" Teri said, swatting at him.

"I think we'll be leaving now," Kyle said, offering his hand to Jessica. "We'll meet back here in an hour."

Lauren ducked out and made a quick detour to the hotel gift shop. If she was going to have a formal dinner with KC, she was going to look her best. Last night she had worn the only nice evening dress she had. It was time to put her Visa to good use for this emergency.

The sales clerk directed her to a rack of semi-formal wear at the back of the shop. Filing through quickly, Lauren selected every dress in her size and slipped into the dressing room. She had just put on the first one when she heard familiar voices outside the slatted changing room door.

"And you're telling me you don't know her name?" Kyle's voice asked.

"I only know her as Wren," Kenton answered.

"May I help you find something?" the clerk asked.

"Yes," Kyle answered. "We need something for sunburn and a coat and tie for this guy."

"Those are along the back wall. The lotions are over there."

"Thanks. So, what are you going to do?" Lauren could hear them coming closer. She tried to peek through the slats.

"I wish I knew," Kenton's voice sounded rich and deep, exactly as she had imagined it. "Do you know what it's like to have your heart ripped out, and the woman you love vanish?"

Lauren bit her lip and felt the tears welling up in her eyes.

"Yeah, I do," Kyle's voice sounded tight. Lauren thought of Lindsay and her inscription in *Pilgrim's Progress*.

There was a pause before Kenton said, "I guess you do." Now Kenton sounded choked up. "Wren was the other half of me, Kyle. She held the other half of my heart in her hand, and I don't know where she is. I called all the hospitals in Portland asking if there had been any car accidents involving twenty-five-year-old women in rental cars. Is that crazy, or what? There weren't any, but I was determined to find her. I'm going to find her, too."

"What if she doesn't want to be found?" Kyle asked. "You like skinny or fat?"

"I don't care if she's skinny or fat or one-eyed! It's her soul I fell in love with."

"I was asking about ties," Kyle said. "There are four black ones here. Do you like skinny or fat ties?"

"That one," Kenton said.

"Here. Try on this jacket. If it doesn't work, I have one you can borrow." There was a pause with some rustling sounds, and then Kyle said, "That's not going to work."

"Are there any others?"

"Doesn't look like it. You can borrow my black one."

"I guess I'm destined to live my whole life off of your hand-me-downs."

"That's what you get for being born last," Kyle teased. "You know, I have to say something. I hear what you're telling me about this woman, Wren. I'm sure she's a nice person, and there's some logical explanation for why she didn't show up. She could have ended up in Fairbanks, even! That's what happened to Lauren on her way to Gordon and

Teri's wedding. And speaking of Lauren, I wish you two hadn't gotten off on the wrong foot. I think she's terrific."

"You search and rescue guys always go for the swooners."

Lauren's heart sank. Kenton's opinion of her, the real her, was obviously not very high.

"I think you would like her, if you gave her a chance," Kyle said. "Jessica told me she's coming off of an unresolved relationship and —"

"Will you kindly listen to what I'm saying?" Kenton said. "You're not paying attention. I'm deeply in love with Wren. I couldn't think of even looking at another woman." They moved past her dressing room, and Lauren held her breath, watching his shadow pass by.

"Is that all, sir?" the clerk asked.

"Yes. And this bottle of sunburn soother. Oh, and can you add a couple of these Dove chocolate bars? My wife has a thing for Dove bars. Our baby will probably be born with wings."

"Either that or it'll come out with acne," Kenton said dryly.

Their voices trailed off as they left the shop. Lauren had been leaning against the slatted door so hard as she strained to hear them that it suddenly popped open, and she nearly spilled out onto the floor.

"Do you need some help back there?"

Lauren caught herself and closed the door. "No, I'm fine, thank you — I think," she muttered under her breath. She quickly tried on the next dress and nearly laughed aloud. It resembled the silver dress Mindy had worn to Leon's birthday party at Jake's.

"Definitely not!" Lauren told herself. Her hands were

shaking as she tried on the next three. She settled happily on a simple black one that made her feel elegant, even with the sand in her hair.

Back in her room she kicked into high gear, showering and dressing. She paid extra attention to every detail. Attaching her small diamond stud earring, she discovered more sand in her ear that the shower hadn't found. Just then there came a quick knock on the door.

Oh, no! They're ready and I'm not!

She scurried to the door in her bare feet and opened it to a hotel staff person who held out to her a perfect white gardenia tucked in a clear florist box.

"Compliments of Mr. Buchanan," he said.

"Thank you," Lauren said, receiving the single, exceptional flower and searching for a card. As the man turned to leave, she asked, "Excuse me. Do you happen to know which Mr. Buchanan?"

The man smiled and shook his head. "No ma'am."

Thirty

Of course it's from Kyle, Lauren reasoned as she returned to the bathroom and pinned the gardenia to her new dress. *Why would it be from Kenton? He thinks I'm a swooner. Kyle probably bought one for each of the women.*

The contrast of the white gardenia on her black dress was stunning. She felt stunning. Her face looked tanned with a splash of sunburn pink across her cheeks. Her eyes were clear and bluer than usual because of her tan. Her hair had cooperated nicely: bangs, thin and billowy across her forehead; the usual fly-away strand tucked neatly behind her ear. And best of all, she felt great inside. *You did this, didn't you, Father? You brought him here, and you're going to work everything out. I know you are.*

Entering the great room a few minutes late, Lauren noticed the others already there, seated in the same area where they had been an hour ago. Only everything was different. Instead of a bunch of beach bums, they all looked like guests on *Lifestyles of the Rich and Famous.*

Kenton was the first to see her. He rose to his feet. Was that a look of astonishment on his face? Delight? Before she could get an accurate reading, he looked away. Kyle and Gordon also rose, and Gordon was the first to speak. "My, don't you clean up nicely!"

Teri looked gorgeous in her new-bride glow. It didn't matter that she had on the same apricot-colored dress she had worn to dinner the night before. Without makeup and with her hair down, flowing freely over her shoulders, she could take on any mermaid in the sea.

Jessica wore a stunning two-piece royal blue outfit and sat with her feet on the footstool and that peaceful expression on her face, looking even more royal than this afternoon. Both Jessica and Teri wore gardenias identical to Lauren's.

"Shall we?" Kyle said, standing before his wife and offering her his arm. He wore a white dinner jacket. Kenton wore the black one with a white shirt and the new black tie. He hung back, letting the two married couples proceed to the dining room arm in arm.

Look at me! Come on KC, offer me your arm.

But he didn't. Without making eye contact with Lauren, he motioned for her to walk ahead of him. So, single file, they trailed the others into the dining room. Their table was waiting in the corner. The husbands pulled out chairs for their wives, and Kenton did the same for Lauren. She was seated across from him at the rectangular table.

"Thanks for the gardenia, Kyle," Lauren said once they were all seated. "It's beautiful."

"You're welcome."

"Aren't they beautiful?" Jessica said. "I love the way gardenias smell."

Lauren glanced over at Kenton, and as she did, he immediately looked down at his menu. Her heart sank. She wanted him to look at her, to smile at her, to talk to her, to fall in love with her the way she had fallen in love with him in writing and now in person.

Yet the entire meal he wouldn't look at her. She would feel his gaze on her, but the moment she would try to make eye contact, he would glance away.

The conversation flowed in and around them like bright Maypole ribbons crossing each other. Just when it seemed an opening presented itself for her to reveal her identity to him, the Maypole dancers would turn the opposite direction, and the previously woven ribbons of thought would come undone.

Finally she turned to him and said, "What's your middle name?"

He looked at her and appeared to be caught, unable to pull away from her gaze, even though he appeared to try. "My middle name?"

Lauren nodded, and the others were silent, curious over her unusual question.

"Carlyle," he said.

A smile danced across her moist lips as she repeated, "Kenton Carlyle." Neither of those names were on her list of possibilities in her notebook. It was the first time she had said his name aloud, and the sense of connectedness, the mystery solved, pulsated through her, infusing her with wild hope and anticipation. Now what should she say?

The waiter appeared, displaying the dessert tray and taking their orders. When he came to Lauren she said, "I'd like some Irish Breakfast tea. That's all."

She cast a subtle glance at Kenton as he said, "I'll have the same." He caught her eye but again refused to really look at her.

The tea arrived. As the others chatted, Lauren meticulously poured enough cream into her cup to just cover the bottom, then tore open a packet of cane sugar and poured half of it into her cup. She watched Kenton's wonderful, strong, smooth hands out of the corner of her eye as he poured the whole packet of sugar directly into the teapot and added the cream after the tea was poured into his cup. She knew he had been watching her hands as well. How many times over the past year had they each gone through this tandem ritual across the miles?

Pouring the amber tea into her cup, Lauren drew up all her courage and, looking across the table, she said, "Kenton?"

Instead of answering, he stood, his head turned away from her, and said, "Excuse me." Then smoothly and swiftly, he disappeared.

Lauren felt as if the wind had been knocked out of her. A familiar fear began to edge its way to the center of her heart; the fear that once he knew who she was, he would leave her. And now, when he didn't even know her yet, he already had left. Lauren felt her hopeful heart shriveling up inside her. KC may have fallen in love with Wren, but Kenton obviously had no room in his heart for Lauren the swooner.

Thirty-One

W here's my brother?" Kyle asked nearly five minutes after Kenton had left the table. "Is he making phone calls? I don't think I've eaten an entire meal with him once in the past eight years without his beeper going off."

Lauren had waited quietly, sipping her tea. Crazy, uncontrolled emotions ripped about inside her. One moment she was ready to run from the dining room, catch a cab to the airport, and leave everyone and everything behind. The next moment she wanted to run though the hotel calling for Kenton until she found him. She would wrap her arms around him and beg him never to leave her. Guilt found its way into her tortured mind. *This is what you deserve,* the accusing voice said. *You abandoned him, and now he's left you.* But Kenton didn't know she was the no-show at the falls. She was simply flesh and blood Lauren to him, and he wasn't attracted to her the way she was to him. Perhaps it was better to find out this way.

"Lauren?" Kyle's voice shook her from her waking nightmare. "I meant to tell you that I invited Kenton to join us for golf tomorrow morning. I hope you don't mind."

"Actually," Lauren said, clearing her throat, which had grown suddenly tight, "I think I'd like to sleep in tomorrow morning. Why don't the two of you go ahead?"

"You sure?"

She nodded. "I'm pretty tired. I think I'll turn in early tonight. Thanks for a fabulous day and a delicious dinner."

Kyle and Gordon both rose as she pushed back her chair. "Good night, everyone. I'll see you in the morning."

Lauren didn't encounter Kenton on the way to her room, as she hoped. She spent a long, tortured night, allowing her imagination to run through every possible scenario. Then she remembered something she had read in *My Utmost for His Highest,* the devotional book she and KC had read through together, over the miles. She wished she had the book with her now, or at least her own Bible. All she could remember was something in the first entry they had both read, March 22, about maintaining a heart that burned for God. That's how she had felt that morning in the gazebo. Every emotion had been cleansed and fine-tuned, ready to line up with her heavenly Father's will.

Now, only twelve hours later, her spiritual renewal was being put to the test. Instead of her usual pattern of thinking, worrying, and then stuffing, Lauren knelt in prayer and stayed on her knees, unaware of the time. She read from the hotel Bible, turning again to the Song of Solomon. At last, some time in the dark, still night, she fell asleep.

When the brightness of the new day roused her, Lauren found she had slept until ten. *Good thing I didn't go golfing,* she thought, rubbing her eyes and noticing that the red message light was lit on her phone. Jessica wanted Lauren to know they were all planning to meet in the lobby at eleven and drive down to Manele Bay for the day.

Lauren knew she couldn't spend the day with Kenton and keep her identity a secret. No matter what he thought of her or what happened to their relationship, she had to tell him. It wasn't fair to leave him thinking she had dropped off the face of the earth.

Dressed and determined, Lauren left her room ready to search for him. She found Kyle at the concierge's desk arranging for their dinner that evening at the Manele Bay Hotel.

"Have you seen Kenton?" Lauren asked.

Kyle turned and, when he looked at Lauren, a concerned expression flickered across his face. "Would you mind waiting a minute? I need to talk to you." Turning to the concierge he said, "Okay, six o'clock is great."

"And the reservation is for five people, is that correct?"

Kyle hesitated before saying, "Yes, dinner for five."

Panic filled Lauren. "Did he leave?" she asked Kyle.

Grasping Lauren by the elbow, Kyle directed her to a corner couch in the great room. They sat down, and he faced her.

"Please try to understand this the way I mean it," Kyle began.

"Did he leave the island?"

"Not yet. He's scheduled for the two o'clock flight."

"I have to talk to him."

"It might be better if you didn't," Kyle said. He leaned closer and said, "Kenton is…" Kyle worked to choose the right word. "Overwhelmed right now with a relationship he has with another woman."

"I know," Lauren said.

"That's right. He told you that on the phone at our house, didn't he? But you see, he can't stand to be around you."

Lauren's heart and face fell. She had guessed he wasn't physically attracted to her, but Kyle made it sound as if Kenton found her repulsive. "I didn't know it was that bad."

"It's bad, all right," Kyle said. "He couldn't finish dinner with us last night because he said you had gotten inside his head or something. He didn't sleep at all last night. He said he was afraid he would dream, and it would be you and not this other woman that he would dream about." Kyle shook his head. "My brother is so intensely attracted to you that he's a wreck."

Lauren didn't know what to say. Suddenly it became clear. She had thought Kenton was displeased with her. But in reality, he was drawn to her as strongly as she was to him, only he didn't know she was Wren. By not looking at her or showing any interest in her as Lauren, he was actually being loyal to her as Wren. How could she have been so blind to what she was doing to him? She could play the emotional game because she knew he was KC. How unfair she had been, first leaving him at the falls and now this.

"I want you to know that this is not like my brother at all," Kyle continued. "He's a mess over it. I agreed with him that he should leave today and try to work out whatever he needs to resolve with this other woman. Apparently she's not interested in a relationship with him, but he can't let her go."

"That's not it," Lauren said in a tight whisper. "I love him. He doesn't know who I am. I have to talk to him. Where is he?"

Kyle rose from the couch as Lauren did. "I'm not so sure

you should talk to him. Give him some time. You'll both be living in Glenbrooke. Let him get over this other woman and see what God has for you both this fall."

"You don't understand. I am the other woman!" Lauren pounded her hand against her chest. "I'm Wren!"

Kyle fell back onto the couch. "You're Wren?"

Lauren nodded, the tears beginning to tumble down her cheeks. "I didn't know how to tell him. First I was rude to him on the phone at your house, then when I saw him here, I realized who he was, and I fainted like a complete idiot! I thought he despised me."

Kyle shook his head. "He's desperately in love with you." A smile began to climb up his face. "With both of you."

"I have to find him. Where did he go?"

"Out by the lake. He was trying to avoid you."

Lauren took off running, trying to brush the tears from her eyes as she bolted out the double glass doors facing the back acreage of the hotel grounds. Taking to the garden path, she scurried past the pool where eight or so guests swam and sunned. Kenton wasn't among them. She continued down the path, looking on every bench under the arbor and around the lake. Overhead, late morning clouds had gathered, hiding the sun.

"Where is he?" She felt like the Shulamite woman she had read about in the Song of Solomon who went seeking her beloved. A verse toward the end of that poem came to mind: "Many waters cannot quench love." Perhaps, just perhaps, all the mistakes and mishaps of the past week were not enough to quench their love, which had grown slowly over the past year.

The darkened sky began to rumble. Light drops of warm

rain fell on her as she headed up the garden path toward the wooded hillside. Down the trail to the left, tucked beneath tall foliage, stood the gazebo where she had met with God the day before. The drops turned into pellets, forcing her to run toward the gazebo and take shelter. Just as she reached the opening, a loud boom of thunder echoed from the heavens. She bolted inside, nearly colliding with Kenton.

"Kenton, I didn't see you!" She impulsively wrapped her arms around him in a hug of joy and relief.

He pulled her arms off with his strong hands and looked as if he were in pain. Perhaps the moist drops on his face weren't rain but tears. "Listen," Kenton said, pushing her away, "I know I probably won't say this the right way, but please bear with me. I need to say it."

"No, let me speak," Lauren said. She drew closer to him, and he backed away again, sitting down on the bench circling the inside of the gazebo. She sat down, less than a foot away from him, her heart bursting to tell him she was Wren.

"Let me say what I need to say," Kenton said, looking at her hard in the eyes, honest and real, face to face.

She could hardly breathe.

"I'm having a difficult time being around you. Please don't take this the wrong way. I'll be flat out honest with you because somehow I'm quite sure you can take it. The truth is, I feel drawn to you. Overpoweringly drawn to you."

A flash of lightening was followed by a distant rumble of thunder.

"But you see, I've already given my heart to another, and even though that relationship is..." He shook his head and looked out at the wild bird of paradise blooming around them. "It's at an unusual place right now. But that doesn't matter. The fact is, I'm not free. Do you understand what I'm saying?"

Lauren dearly wanted to reach over and touch his troubled face or take his hand in hers. She sat still, her hands in her lap, with an honest and peaceful look on her face. "I understand. Now may I tell you something?" She paused. Her mind had gone blank, and all she could say was, "It's me!"

Kenton looked as if he had no idea what she was talking about.

Lauren realized she had had time to put all the pieces together. She needed to unveil the truth slowly so Kenton would have time to absorb the unbelievable truth of their situation.

She rose and walked to the center of the gazebo. "Did you know," she began, her voice faltering, "that sometimes, if you speak directly into the center of a gazebo like this, you can hear an echo? If it's a good echo, you have a hard time telling the echo from the original source."

The rain came down harder. Lauren raised her voice.

"Yesterday, right here, I settled some things with God. You see, for a lot of years, I've been listening to echoes in my life and thinking they were truth. But now I know the true source is always God." She stood still, watching Kenton's expression, which was still clouded.

She grasped her hands together and drew them to her mouth. She realized she was softly crying. "I'm not saying this the way I want to. Let me try to put the pieces together for you. You were the one who introduced me to Irish Breakfast tea. I share your friendship with Robert and Elizabeth Browning. I love playing volleyball. Last summer I bought a kitten at a garage sale, remember?"

An expression of faint understanding mixed with wild confusion ran across Kenton's face. She wondered if maybe the kitten was a poor clue; he might not remember.

Drawing in a deep breath, she said, "KC, it's me. I'm Wren."

For a moment, Kenton didn't move. He didn't blink. He didn't seem to breathe. Then slowly he rose to his feet and came toward her.

"I'm so sorry I left you at the waterfall," she said, the words tumbling out in a jumble. "I know you must be furious at me for leaving you like that. I was scared. I was afraid of so many things. And then I yelled at you on the phone and hung up, and then when I saw you here, I realized it was you, and I don't know what happened. I just fainted. I wouldn't blame you if you despised me after everything I did."

Kenton now stood before her, only inches away, with tears in his eyes. He shook his head, wiping her tears with his thumb. "I could never despise you," he whispered. "You are the other half of my heart."

Lauren reached her quivering hand up to his strong jaw and caught his runaway tears, feeling the coarse stubble across his chin.

He grasped her hand and, pressing it against his cheek, gently kissed each finger. "I am and always will be yours. Do you know I would have searched for you for the rest of my life? I was frantic with worry."

"I'm sorry," she began.

He silenced her by closing his eyes and giving a slight shake of his head. "All is forgiven. I understand."

Lauren felt a huge weight lifting from her. It dawned on her that they were finally together. How many times had she dreamed of meeting KC face to face? Of looking into his eyes and feeling his arms around her? It had never been like this in her vivid imaginings that obviously were not as creative as God's. *This,* she decided, *is what falling in love is supposed to feel like.*

Kenton didn't seem to be able to take his eyes off of her. "You are even more beautiful than I dared to think." The rain now fell in soft whispers.

Lauren's eyes scanned his face, memorizing every curve. "You are more everything than I dared to think. Are you sure you're not disappointed in me?"

"Disappointed?" Kenton threw back his head, and a deep, rumbling laugh rose from his chest and spilled out his lips. It was the first time she had heard him laugh, and she loved it, just as she loved everything about him. "Never," he said, looking into her eyes. A solemnity returned to his gaze as he said, "You are my echo, Wren."

Their eyes seemed to shoot electronic messages back and forth. She imagined he was asking if she wanted to be kissed. Her silent message back to him was, "More than you will ever know!"

But instead of bending to kiss her, Kenton surprised her by going down on one knee. Taking her hands in his, he spoke in a voice rich with emotion. "Lauren…" Then he stopped and said, "What's your last name?"

Lauren playfully put her hand on her hip and said, "Phillips. Lauren Michelle Phillips. If you're going to have the boldness to address a woman on your knees, you should at least know her last name!"

Kenton laughed warmly and reached for her hand before she could wiggle away from him. With a tender seriousness returning to his face, he said, "Lauren Michelle Phillips, my Wren, will you marry me?"

Lauren followed the impulse of her heart and went down on her knees so that she was facing him at eye level. "Kenton Carlyle Buchanan, my KC, my answer is..." She squeezed his hands tighter. "No."

"No?" he echoed.

"No."

He looked as if he had just had the wind knocked out of him.

"Kenton," she said, drawing his strong hands to her lips and kissing the fingers that had brought his words to her heart. "You only know part of me."

"I know your heart," he said.

"And I know yours."

"What else is there to know, Wren?"

"The rest of me. And for me to know the rest of you. We know each other on the inside already. I think we need to take some time to get to know each other on the outside. KC and Wren need to spend time with Lauren and Kenton before they make any promises to each other."

"Beautiful and wise," Kenton said, rising to his feet and pulling Lauren up with him. "You're right. That's what we'll do. We'll give ourselves time to get to know each other 'in real life.' Convenient, isn't it, how God is moving both of us to Glenbrooke in a month?"

"Convenient," she murmured. Her silent invitation for that kiss flashed once again from her eyes.

Kenton let his affectionate gaze cover Lauren. She felt a

veil of invisible peace on her face as she tilted it up toward him. He drew in a deep breath and placed his hand behind her head, weaving his fingers gently in her hair. With the other hand he traced her lips with his forefinger, his eyes studying each curve as if to memorize it for an exam.

"'How say you?'" he whispered the familiar Browning line. "'Let us, O my dove, Let us be unashamed of soul, As earth lies bare to heaven above! How is it under our control, To love or not to love?'" Before the last word was out of his mouth, his lips had met hers in a lingering kiss that was full of love.

As they slowly drew apart, the sun returned, immersing their gazebo in glimmering crystals of light. Lauren breathed into his ear a line from Elizabeth's sonnet that she had memorized months ago, hoping it would one day come true with KC. "'And I who looked for only God, found thee! I find thee; I am safe, and strong and glad.'"

Kenton wrapped his arms around his Wren and drew her head to his chest where, for the first time, she heard with her own ears the beating of his oh-so-familiar heart.

Dear Reader:

Last spring I found a treasure: two volumes of *The Letters of Robert Browning and Elizabeth Barrett Browning,* bearing a copyright of 1899. These unassuming books, each nearly two inches thick, were tucked away on a dusty shelf in a used bookstore. What had caught my attention was the beautifully embossed gold trim on the faded green covers.

I took them home, sat down with a knife (many of the pages weren't cut yet), and opened to Robert's first letter to Elizabeth, written January 10, 1845. It began, "I love your verses with all my heart, dear Miss Barrett, and this is no off-hand complimentary letter that I shall write."

I was hooked. For days, and then weeks, I peeked over the shoulders of first Robert and then Elizabeth as they crafted words with quill and ink and trusted the London postal service to return the echo of each other's hearts. After more than a year of nearly daily correspondence, they eloped and stole away to Italy, where Elizabeth, a thirty-nine-year-old invalid, was in many ways given a second lease on life. For almost sixteen years she lived under the canopy of Robert's adoring love. She even gave birth to a son at the age of forty-three.

In her *Sonnets of the Portuguese,* Elizabeth wrote:

Unlike are we, unlike, O princely Heart!
Unlike our uses and our destinies.
Our ministering two angels look surprise
On one another, as they strike athwart
Their wings in passing.

What do you think? Do "ministering angels" still pass each other with surprise as God brings together two unlikely people? I think so. That's why it was easy to write the story of Kenton and Lauren.

In a grander sense, I believe that's what happens with us and Christ. We're his bride. He has written his love letters to us and trusted the Holy Spirit to deliver them to our hearts. He woos us, patiently waiting for the day when we will be completely his, and we can steal away to the place he has prepared for us.

Let us then be unashamed of our souls. Let us love him and each other with abandon. And may we say, when his love canopies us, giving us a second lease on life, "I am safe, and strong, and glad."

Always,

Robin Jones Gunn

A P.S. from Robin:

Thanks for all the letters you've been sending! I'm delighted to hear from so many moms who say they're glad they can share these Palisades Pure Romance novels with their teenage daughters.

It occurred to me that some of these readers might get the impression from this story that it's good and/or safe to try "surfing the Net" in hopes of finding someone like the hero of this book, KC.

Perhaps it goes without saying, but the newspapers are full of tragic, true accounts of young people who have been taken advantage of through such Internet connections.

Echoes is, of course, completely fictional.

So to all my young-hearted readers, if your mom hasn't told you already, I will. *Don't try this at home!*

PALISADES...PURE ROMANCE

= PALISADES <

Reunion, Karen Ball
Refuge, Lisa Tawn Bergren
Torchlight, Lisa Tawn Bergren
Treasure, Lisa Tawn Bergren
Chosen, Lisa Tawn Bergren
Firestorm, Lisa Tawn Bergren
Cherish, Constance Colson
Angel Valley, Peggy Darty
Seascape, Peggy Darty
Sundance, Peggy Darty
Love Song, Sharon Gillenwater
Antiques, Sharon Gillenwater
Secrets, Robin Jones Gunn
Whispers, Robin Jones Gunn
Echoes, Robin Jones Gunn
Coming Home, Barbara Jean Hicks
Glory, Marilyn Kok
Sierra, Shari MacDonald
Forget-Me-Not, Shari MacDonald
Diamonds, Shari MacDonald
Westward, Amanda MacLean
Stonehaven, Amanda MacLean
Everlasting, Amanda MacLean
Betrayed, Lorena McCourtney
Escape, Lorena McCourtney
Voyage, Elaine Schulte
A Christmas Joy, Darty, Gillenwater, MacLean
Mistletoe, Ball, Hicks, McCourtney

THE PALISADES LINE

Ask for them at your local bookstore. If the title you seek is not in stock,
the store may order you a copy using the ISBN listed.

Reunion, Karen Ball (July, 1996)
ISBN 0-88070-951-0
There are wolves on Taylor Sorensen's ranch. Wildlife biologist Connor Alexander is sure of it. So he takes a job as a ranch hand to prove it. Soon he and Taylor are caught in a fierce controversy—and in a determined battle against the growing attraction between them...an attraction that neither can ignore.

Chosen, Lisa Tawn Bergren
ISBN 0-88070-768-2
When biblical archeologist Alexsana Rourke is handed the unprecedented honor of excavating Solomon's Stables in Jerusalem, she has no idea that she'll need to rely heavily upon the new man in her life—CNN correspondent Ridge McIntyre—and God, to save her.

Refuge, Lisa Tawn Bergren
ISBN 0-88070-875-1 (New ISBN)
Part One: A Montana rancher and a San Francisco marketing exec—only one incredible summer and God could bring such diverse lives together. *Part Two:* Lost and alone, Emily Walker needs and wants a new home, a sense of family. Can one man lead her to the greatest Father she could ever want and a life full of love?

Firestorm, Lisa Tawn Bergren (October, 1996)
ISBN 0-88070-953-7
In the sequel to Bergren's best-selling *Refuge*, *Firestorm* tells the romantic tale of two unlikely soulmates: a woman who fears fire, and the man who loves it. Reyne Oldre wasn't always afraid, but a tragic accident one summer changed her forever. Can Reyne get beyond her fear and give her heart to smoke jumper Logan Quinn?

Torchlight, Lisa Tawn Bergren
ISBN 0-88070-806-9
When beautiful heiress Julia Rierdon returns to Maine to remodel her family's estate, she finds herself torn between the man she plans to marry and unexpected feelings for a mysterious wanderer who threatens to steal her heart.

Treasure, Lisa Tawn Bergren
ISBN 0-88070-725-9

She arrived on the Caribbean island of Robert's Foe armed with a lifelong dream—to find her ancestor's sunken ship—and yet the only man who can help her stands stubbornly in her way. Can Christina and Mitch find their way to the ship *and* to each other?

Cherish, Constance Colson
ISBN 0-88070-802-6

Recovering from the heartbreak of a failed engagement, Rose Anson seeks refuge at a resort on Singing Pines Island, where she plans to spend a peaceful summer studying and painting the spectacular scenery of international Lake of the Woods. But when a flamboyant Canadian and a big-hearted American compete for her love, the young artist must face her past—and her future. What follows is a search for the source and meaning of true love: a journey that begins in the heart and concludes in the soul.

Angel Valley, Peggy Darty
ISBN 0-88070-778-X

When teacher Laurel Hollingsworth accepts a summer tutoring position for a wealthy socialite family, she faces an enormous challenge in her young student, Anna Lee Wentworth. However, the real challenge is ahead of her: hanging on to her heart when older brother Matthew Wentworth comes to visit. Soon Laurel and Matthew find that they share a faith in God...and powerful feelings for one another. Can Laurel and Matthew find time to explore their relationship while she helps the emotionally troubled Anna Lee and fights to defend her love for the beautiful *Angel Valley*?

Seascape, Peggy Darty
ISBN 0-88070-927-8

On a pristine sugar sand beach in Florida, Jessica has a lot to reflect upon. The untimely death of her husband, Blake...and the sudden entrance of a new man, distracting her from her grief. In the midst of opening a B&B, can Jessica overcome her anger and forgive the one responsible for Blake's death? Loving the mysterious new man in her life will depend upon it.

Sundance, Peggy Darty (August, 1996)
ISBN 0-88070-952-9

Follow Ginger Grayson to the wilds of British Columbia, Canada, where she meets Craig Cameron, a widowed rancher with two small sons who desperately need a mother. Is free-spirited Ginger ready to settle down in the 1990's last wild frontier? And can Craig risk his heart again, all the while wondering if Ginger can handle his rugged lifestyle?

Love Song, Sharon Gillenwater
ISBN 0-88070-747-X

When famous country singer Andrea Carson returns to her hometown to recuperate from a life-threatening illness, she seeks nothing more than a respite from the demands of stardom that have sapped her creativity and ability to perform. It's Andi's old high school friend, Wade Jamison, who helps her to realize that she needs inner healing as well. As Andi's strength grows, so do her feelings for the rancher who has captured her heart. But can their relationship withstand the demands of her career? Or will their romance be as fleeting as a beautiful *Love Song*?

Antiques, Sharon Gillenwater
ISBN 0-88070-801-8

Deeply wounded by the infidelity of his wife, widower Grant Adams swore off all women—until meeting charming antiques dealer Dawn Carson. Although he is drawn to her, Grant struggles to trust again. Dawn finds herself overwhelmingly attracted to the darkly brooding cowboy, but won't marry a nonbeliever. As Grant learns more about her faith, he is touched by its impact on her life and slowly begins to trust.

Echoes, Robin Jones Gunn
ISBN 0-88070-773-9

In this dramatic romance filled with humor, Lauren Phillips enters the wild, uncharted territory of the Internet on her home computer and "connects" with a man known only as "KC." Recovering from a broken engagement and studying for her teaching credential, her correspondence with KC becomes the thing she enjoys most. Will their e-mail romance become a true love story when they meet face to face?

Secrets, Robin Jones Gunn
ISBN 0-88070-721-6

Seeking a new life as an English teacher in a peaceful Oregon town, Jessica tries desperately to hide the details of her identity from the community...until she falls in love. Will the past keep Jessica and Kyle apart forever?

Whispers, Robin Jones Gunn
ISBN 0-88070-755-0

Teri Moreno went to Maui eager to rekindle a romance. But when circumstances turn out to be quite different than she expects, she finds herself spending a great deal of time with a handsome, old high school crush who now works at a local resort. But the situation becomes more complicated when Teri meets Gordon, a clumsy, endearing Australian with a wild past, and both men begin to pursue her. Will Teri respond to God's gentle urgings toward true love? The answer lies in her response to the gentle *Whispers* in her heart.

Coming Home, Barbara Hicks
ISBN 0-88070-945-6
Keith Castle is running from a family revelation that destroyed his world, and deeply hurt his heart. Katie Brannigan is the childhood friend who was wounded by his sudden disappearance. Together, Keith and Katie could find healing and learn that in his own time, God manages all things for good. But can Katie bring herself to give love one more chance?

Glory, Marilyn Kok
ISBN 0-88070-754-2
To Mariel Forrest, the teaching position in Taiwan provided more than a simple escape from grief; it also offered an opportunity to deal with her feelings toward the God she once loved, but ultimately blamed for the death of her family. Once there, Mariel dares to ask the timeless question: "If God is good, why do we suffer?" What follows is an inspiring story of love, healing, and renewed confidence in God's goodness.

Diamonds, Shari MacDonald (November, 1996)
ISBN 0-88070-982-0
When spirited sports caster Casey Foster inherits a minor league team, she soon discovers that baseball isn't all fun and games. Soon, Casey is juggling crazy promotional events, major league expectations, and egos of players like Tucker Boyd: a pitcher who wants nothing more than to return to the major leagues...until Casey captures his heart and makes him see diamonds in a whole new way.

Forget-Me-Not, Shari MacDonald
ISBN 0-88070-769-0
Traveling to England's famed Newhaven estate to pursue an internship as a landscape architect, Hayley Buckman looked forward to making her long-held career dreams come true. But upon arrival, Hayley is quickly drawn to the estate and its mysterious inhabitants, despite a sinister warning urging her to leave. Will an endearing stranger help her solve the mystery and find love as well?

Sierra, Shari MacDonald
ISBN 0-88070-726-7
When spirited photographer Celia Randall travels to eastern California for a short-term assignment, she quickly is drawn to—and locks horns with—editor Marcus Stratton. Will lingering heartaches destroy Celia's chance at true love? Or can she find hope and healing high in the Sierra?

Westward, Amanda MacLean
ISBN 0-88070-751-8
Running from a desperate fate in the South toward an unknown future in the West, plantation-born artist Juliana St. Clair finds herself torn between two men, one an undercover agent with a heart of gold, the other a man with evil intentions and a smooth facade. Witness Juliana's dangerous travels toward faith and love as she follows God's lead in this powerful historical novel.

Stonehaven, Amanda MacLean
ISBN 0-88070-757-7
Picking up in the years following Westward, Stonehaven follows Callie St. Clair back to the South where she has returned to reclaim her ancestral home. As she works to win back the plantation, the beautiful and dauntless Callie turns it into a station on the Underground Railroad. Covering her actions by playing the role of a Southern belle, Callie risks losing Hawk, the only man she has ever loved. Readers will find themselves quickly drawn into this fast-paced novel of treachery, intrigue, spiritual discovery, and unexpected love.

Everlasting, Amanda MacLean
ISBN 0-88070-929-4
Picking up where the captivating Stonehaven left off, Everlasting brings readers face to face once more with charming, courageous—and very Irish—Sheridan O'Brian. Will she find her missing twin? And will Marcus Jade, a reporter bent on finding out what really happened to Shamus, destroy his chances with her by being less than honest?

Betrayed, Lorena McCourtney
ISBN 0-88070-756-9
As part of a wealthy midwestern family, young Rosalyn Fallon was sheltered from the struggles brought on by the Depression. But after the collapse of her father's company and the elopement of her fiancé and best friend, Rosalyn unexpectedly finds herself facing both hardship and heartbreak. Will her new life out West and a man as rugged and rough as the land itself help her recover?

Escape, Lorena McCourtney (September, 1996)
ISBN 1-57673-012-3
Is money really everything? The winsome Beth Curtis must come to terms with that question as she fights to hold on to guardianship of her nephew, even facing her deceased sister-in-law's brother. Sent to collect the boy, handsome Guy Wilkerson has no idea that he will fall for Beth, and come to see his own family's ways of living in a new light. Can the two overcome such diversity to be together, beginning their own family?

Voyage, Elaine Schulte (August, 1996)
ISBN 1-57673-011-5

Traveling via ship to the Holy Land, Ann Marie is on a pilgrimage, discovering things about faith and love all the way. But will a charming man who guides her—among the romantic streets of Greece and elsewhere—distract her from the One who truly loves her?

A Christmas Joy, MacLean, Darty, Gillenwater
ISBN 0-88070-780-1 (same length as other Palisades books)

Snow falls, hearts change, and love prevails! In this compilation, three experienced Palisades authors spin three separate novelettes centering around the Christmas season and message.

By Amanda MacLean: A Christmas pageant coordinator in a remote mountain village of Northern California is reunited with an old friend and discovers the greatest gift of all.

By Peggy Darty: A college ski club reunion brings together model Heather Grant and an old flame. Will they gain a new understanding?

By Sharon Gillenwater: A chance meeting in an airport that neither of them could forget...and a Christmas reunion.

Mistletoe: Ball, Hicks, McCourtney (October, 1996)
ISBN 1-57673-013-1

A new Christmas anthology of three novellas...all in one keepsake book!

❧

Also look for our new line:

PALISADES PREMIER
More Story. More Romance.

Chase the Dream, Constance Colson
ISBN 0-88070-928-6, $11.99

Alison Austin's childhood dream of being a world-champion barrel racer leads to problems at home and in the arena. Rising rodeo star Forrest Jackson, wounded from the death of his father and abandonment of his mother, is Alison's ideal—and her cousin Jenny's boyfriend. Ultimately, Alison must decide how much she is willing to give up...and to take.

Raised on the circuit, Jenny's love for Forrest is mixed with her love for barrel racing, while bull rider Tom Rawlings rodeos with much different motives.

As the time runs down and the competition heightens, the destinies of these four entwine, leading to a breathless climax. It's rodeo: the rough-and-tumble sport propelled by dreams; where love, life, and death are separated by mere seconds; and where meeting the Master Rider is inevitable.

Promise Me the Dawn, **Amanda MacLean (September, 1996)**
ISBN 0-88070-955-3, $11.99

Set in turn-of-the-century San Francisco and Monterey, *Promise Me the Dawn* weaves the tender love story of spirited English beauty Molly Quinn and Zachary MacAlister, an immigrant who came to America to flee his family's titles, wealth, and influence. During the dark days that follow the 1906 earthquake, Molly and Zachary plan a future rendezvous in the Pacific cliffs.

After they separate, Molly makes a name for herself and becomes the glamorous, new toast of the town. When Zach proposes, Molly decides that she hasn't lived enough yet, and lets him go. But when she later realizes that she may have lost him for good, Molly must reexamine the desires of her heart and turn back to her God before rediscovering the love she nearly lost in *Promise Me the Dawn.*

‌

⌇

AND ESPECIALLY FOR YOUNG ADULTS:
Announcing the exciting new
Pacific Cascades University Series!

Come and meet nine college students and witness their trials and tribulations as they discover more about relationships, college life, and their world.

Freshman Blues, Wendy Lee Nentwig, ISBN 0-88070-947-2 (July 1996)
Homeward Heart, Lissa Halls Johnson, ISBN 0-88070-948-0 (July 1996)
True Identity, Bernie Sheahan, ISBN 0-88070-949-9 (September 1996)
Spring Break, Wendy Lee Nentwig, ISBN 0-88070-950-2 (September 1996)

Titles subject to change.

If you enjoyed *Echoes*, look for Robin Jones Gunn's *Secrets* and *Whispers!* Below is an excerpt from *Whispers*, Teri and Gordon's love story. Available at your local Christian bookstore.

CHAPTER

One

❦

Teri Moreno flipped her thick brown hair over her shoulder and peered through the cluster of Maui tourists gathered at the airport baggage claim. She had hoped to see Mark among the locals, but it was her sister's voice that greeted her.

"Teri, over here!"

Anita ran toward her with a lei of white plumeria flowers strung over her arm. "You're here!" Anita said breathlessly, giving Teri a hug. "I'm sorry we weren't here to meet your flight. Here, these are for you." She placed the fragrant flowered leis around Teri's neck. "Dan's parking the car. We got a late start. I'm sorry."

"Don't worry about it," Teri said, lifting the sweet flowers to her nose and drawing in the scent. A dozen memories of her previous summer on the island filled her mind. She looked past her sister and with a sheepish smile asked, "Mark wasn't able to come?"

"No, he'll meet us for dinner, though. You really look great!" Anita said, giving Teri's arm a squeeze. "Did you lose some weight?"

Aware that her slim sister's glance had rested on Teri's thighs, Teri said, "Not really." A familiar uneasiness settled in. She had never been able to wear a size six pair of jeans like her older sister could—nor would Teri ever be able to.

"You look great, too," Teri said. "I love your hair like that. I don't think you've ever worn it that short. It's cute."

Anita fingered the ends of her sleek, dark hair that clung to the nape of her neck. "Do you like it? I had it cut a week ago. I'm still getting used to it, but I think I like it. Dan does."

Just then Dan appeared. He was the same age as Anita, twenty-seven. But his dark, wavy hair and short, stocky build gave him the look of a high school wrestler.

"So how was your flight?" Dan said, giving Teri a hug and motioning with his head that they should follow him to the baggage claim area.

"Fine. Uneventful."

"Don't think for a minute that your five weeks here will be uneventful," Anita said. "We are going to have so much fun! I have all kinds of things planned for us."

Teri wondered if Anita had included Mark in her plans. "That's my suitcase," Teri said.

Dan grabbed it for her and lifted it with ease. He had lots of experience with luggage since he worked as a bellhop at the Halekuali'i, one of the most expensive resorts on the west side of Maui. "Is this your only bag?"

"That's it," Teri said.

"Traveling light this time, I see. Looks like you learned all you need to bring to Maui is a bathing suit," Dan said, leading them out to the parking lot.

"A bathing suit and every hard-earned penny I could scrape up," Teri added. She again drew in the sweet scent of the flowers around her neck as they stepped out from under the protected covering of the baggage claim area. A strong wind blew their hair and dried the perspiration from their shirts.

"Ah!" Teri greeted the island breeze with upturned chin and closed eyes. "It's so wonderful to be back here. Do you know how many times I've dreamed of this very moment? Standing here, feeling this wind in my hair, and smelling the flowers." She impulsively gave Anita a hug. "I can't believe I'm here!"

"Why don't you stay for good this time?" Anita asked.

"Don't I wish," Teri said.

"I'm serious. Why don't you move here?"

"Well, one small matter is making a living on the island."

"They always need teachers," Dan said. "The pay isn't great, but you could always do like the rest of us and wait tables on the weekends."

"I don't imagine the demand is high for Spanish teachers," Teri said.

"We can always find out," Dan replied. He unlocked the trunk of their white compact car and dropped her suitcase inside. It had been a rental car that he had bought from a friend for a low price because the right rear door was smashed in. They still hadn't fixed the door. Teri noticed the rust inside the dented area, which hadn't been there a year ago. She slid into the backseat through the one rear door that did work and made a mental note that, even though they both worked two jobs, they hadn't been able to fix their car. How could she possibly afford to support herself in such an expensive location?

"I don't know," Teri said. "I have a comfortable life in

Oregon. Maui is a great place for a vacation, but I don't know if I could actually live here."

"Sure you could," Anita coaxed her.

Dan paid the airport parking lot attendant and pulled out into the traffic.

"Can you wait for dinner or are you starving? You know it will take about an hour to drive to our side of the island and probably another half hour before we eat," Dan said.

"My stomach can wait," Teri answered. The part of her that couldn't wait was her eyes. They longed to feast on the sights of this enchanted paradise. With all the windows down, Dan drove the two-lane highway that linked the two sides of the island. Anita chattered away as they drove, while Teri only half listened. She was too absorbed in the scenery.

First came the waving sugar cane fields in the central valley. To the left rose Haleakala, the great volcano circled in a wreath of clouds that looked like a halo of baby's breath. The road followed the outer rim of the west side of the island, curving through cut volcanic rock and past sequestered sandy coves shaded by palm trees.

Teri drank in the beauty of the blue ocean and the imposing sight of the nearby neighboring islands, popping up out of the Pacific Ocean: Kahoolawe, Lana'i, and the green, sleeping giant, Moloka'i, which lay only nine miles north of Dan and Anita's small house. She had waited a year in rainy Oregon for this feast of her senses, a year filled with romantic dreams and hope inspired speculations. Now Teri Angelina Raquel Moreno was about to see if those dreams were ready to come true.